Windsor in Watercolour

A walk through history

by Jeff Sanderson

Curfew Publishing

An Illustrated Journey through the
Historic Streets and Parkland of Windsor

To my family, friends and everyone
who has given me so much encouragement
to make this book a reality

Contents

The Views

Windsor — a personal viewpoint

I have been fond of Windsor since my first visit at about the age of ten and have never tired of it. Brought up in Streatham, South London in the 1950s it was not often that my brothers and I got to see places out in the countryside, as Windsor seemed to be in those days. We first visited the area by train soon after my uncle, an aircraft engineer, changed his work location from the old London airport at Croydon (Surrey) to the expanding new one at Heathrow. He and his family moved to Englefield Green, a village about 5 miles (8 Km) away from Windsor and on Sunday visits we sometimes went to the nearby Great Park and occasionally to Windsor Town. I learnt to ride a bicycle in the Great Park using a bike borrowed from one of my cousins.

Being a castle fan from an early age I was impressed with the grandeur of Windsor though was aware that it had been altered a lot over the years, quite different to the romantic ruins I was used to. I have one particular memory. Anyone who has listened to the classic 1950s radio episode 'Sunday Afternoon at Home' by comedian Tony Hancock will be reminded that in that decade Britain was virtually closed on Sundays. Windsor, though a tourist town, was no exception. On one Sunday visit I had been promised fish and chips for lunch. Sadly we discovered that there were no fish and chips to be had and as a substitute I was given a bun. In a fit of pique I hurled my bun into the river, so depriving myself of any sustenance but no doubt pleasing the ducks. On a Sunday visit today one could probably purchase fish and chips in at least twenty establishments and find most world cuisines on offer.

My family also migrated to Englefield Green when I was 17 and I moved to Windsor in 1982. I had passed my O-level in art and though school reports indicated I had some aptitude I ended up as a scientist with a degree in Zoology. However I was lucky in that the courses in Zoology and Botany (which I also studied) required a great deal of accurate drawing of specimens. I probably did more drawing than most art students. From then on I dabbled with watercolour, oil and acrylic painting occasionally but did not take up drawing again until the late 1980s when I joined a life drawing class. I enjoyed the challenges this brought and carried on for several years but then in the mid 1990s tried my hand at drawing a street scene, the first being in Eton. From that moment I conceived the idea of creating a series of views to cover the whole of Windsor and Eton with some buildings inevitably being drawn several times from different angles. With one exception all the views in this book were drawn from life which I find enjoyable, but since the advent of digital photography I now occasionally save time by using reference photographs to fill in repetitive details such as windows. Standing in the street drawing can be a bit daunting at first but gets easier over time. The paintings were all done in the studio using photographs displayed on a laptop, and more recently an iPad, as a reference for colour and shadows and to populate the views.

I carried on drawing and painting for many years with little thought to the practicalities of writing notes to accompany my views. I considered getting some help but ended up writing them myself. Coming to the subject as a relative layman I soon realised how woefully ignorant I was of the finer detail of Windsor's history even though I had bought and read several local books over the years. After a lot of study in Windsor Reference Library and the discovery of many useful websites I gradually began to piece it together. The technology and increased communication of the digital age has been invaluable even though the artwork itself is still very much in a traditional format. My new knowledge has taught me how much more fulfilling it is to find out the story behind the buildings and streets and has given me a greater interest in British history in general.

A Brief History of Windsor Castle
(with notes on the town)

The town of Windsor owes its existence to the castle and the castle would not exist were it not for the aspirations of William of Normandy (The Conqueror). The invasion of England by William in 1066 was not without reason or purely for the gain of lands and power; he had apparently been promised the throne of England by the Anglo-Saxon King, **Edward the Confessor** in about 1051. William's wife, Matilda, was a direct descendant of Alfred the Great who ruled much of England from 871-899. However, when Edward died in January 1066 his brother-in-law Harold Godwinson was elected King, as **Harold II**. Harold very soon found himself besieged by claims to the English throne from both the King of Norway and William of Normandy. He successfully beat off the Norwegians at Stamford Bridge (near York) in September but his army then had to rush to Sussex to take on the Normans. It is perhaps not surprising that Harold's capable but tired troops were defeated by a well-trained force using mounted knights and skilled archers in addition to foot soldiers. The Battle of Hastings in October 1066 was decisive and led to **William I** (Norman) being crowned King of England on Christmas Day.

Prior to 1066 true castles were virtually unknown in England; Roman forts and other pre-Norman fortifications were communal and not the private fortified dwelling of a King or Lord, by which the castle is defined. Castles, including those made from stone, were well known in northern Europe and from the outset the Normans introduced to England the 'motte and bailey', a standardised design which could be built quickly using local timber and relatively unskilled labour. These established secure bases from which troops could control the local population and by about 1070 a ring of such castles was built around London, all within a day's march (about 20 miles/32 km) from the capital and from each other. Windsor was one of these.

The site chosen for this castle was a chalk outcrop (an outlying fragment of the Chiltern Hills) close to the River Thames in the manor of Clewer, on land that William had given to one of his Norman Lords but now had to rent back for 12 shillings a year, a payment which continued until the 1500s. It proved an ideal location, well placed geographically as part of the ring, good connection by river to London and close to an existing riverside Saxon palace/hunting lodge with good sport to be had in the surrounding countryside. This riverside palace, which had been used by Saxon kings including Edward the Confessor, was about 2 miles (3.5 km) downstream at a place called Windlesora, a name later shortened to Windsor.

Most motte and bailey castles consisted of a high artificial flat-topped mound (motte) surrounded by a ditch on which was erected a wooden palisade or possibly a tower – a defensible place of refuge and a lookout. The material dug out to create the ditch was used to form the mound. Surrounding (or next to) the motte was a much larger living space (bailey) also protected by a wooden palisade and a ditch. The majority of such castles had one bailey but at Windsor the site lent itself to the creation of two, with the motte and its tower between them. Many of the original wooden motte and bailey castles never progressed beyond this stage and have now disappeared or exist only as earthworks. Some such as Windsor were gradually transformed by the replacement of wood with stone and the addition of towers, gatehouses and substantial living accommodation. The two baileys became known as the Upper and Lower Wards and a small additional Middle Ward was later created around the motte. From the outset the location of Windsor made it popular for Royal hunting and festivals but initially the Saxon palace at Windlesora (now Old Windsor) was used for these functions in preference to the more basic facilities to be found in the nearby castle.

By 1110 **Henry I** (Norman) son of William I, had transferred his court from the Old Windsor palace to the castle at New Windsor following the creation of Royal apartments in the Upper Ward. It is not known for certain whether these were of wood or stone. At about this time the town of New Windsor grew up close to the walls, to serve the needs of the King and his castle. On the opposite side of the Thames was the originally Saxon settlement that evolved into Eton Town.

Henry II (Plantagenet) grandson of Henry I, became King in 1154. In 1170, a century after the castle was created, he began the conversion of the wooden palisades into stone walls. The artificial mound (motte) was now sufficiently compacted to support a stone shell keep. Stone walls were erected around the Upper Ward and the northern side of the Middle and Lower Wards together with private Royal apartments for the King (Upper Ward) and a Great Hall for official functions (Lower Ward). For the outer walls the tough Heath stone, a very durable siliceous sandstone abundant at Bagshot some 10 miles (16 km) south of Windsor, proved an ideal material which was also used in many subsequent building programmes though not always from the same source.

Neither Richard I nor King John (sons of Henry II) made substantial additions though some work continued on improving the fortifications. It was during the reign of John that the castle saw the only damaging siege it has ever endured. John, a greedy tyrant, was unpopular with the barons and in 1215 was pressured by them to accept the Magna Carta, a document that limited the absolute power of the King and gave legal rights and protection to all free men. It was agreed at Runnymede about 4 miles (6 km) from Windsor. In 1216, after John had reneged on this deal, the barons called on Prince Louis of France to bring an army over to assist them. Most castles in the south of England submitted to this force but Windsor held out and never capitulated. John died the same year and his successor the nine year old Henry III became King.

In the reign of **Henry III** (Plantagenet) 1216-72 some building work was done in the early years (Henry III Tower and the Devil's Tower now called Edward III Tower) but the most significant additions were started when he came of age in 1227. The stone fortifications of the western side of the Lower Ward forming the West End Wall, with three large drum shaped towers (now called the Curfew, Garter and Salisbury Towers) and curtain wall between, still retain a formidable appearance. These works completed the replacement of all the original 1070 wooden fortifications with stone and added much more. Damage sustained during the 1216 siege led to repairs to the motte following subsidence and a rebuilding of the Round Tower to a different orientation and with the flattened side that is seen day. Improvements to the Royal apartments and Great Hall were carried out and a new chapel dedicated to St Edward the Confessor built in the Lower Ward.

Edward I (Plantagenet) son of Henry III, who built many great castles in North Wales, did not alter Windsor Castle but raised the status of the town. In 1277 he gave New Windsor its first Charter, making it a Free Borough with control over its own affairs and local government.

Edward III (Plantagenet) was born at Windsor and became king in 1327. Many significant events occurred during his reign including war with Scotland and France, the latter known as the Hundred Years War. Victories in France and money gained from ransoms allowed him to spend lavishly on Windsor Castle. He was inspired by the idea of chivalry and brotherhood among knights and in 1344 began to create a building to house a giant Round Table similar to that of the legendary King Arthur. This project was abandoned but the basic concept revived in 1348 with the foundation of the Order of the Garter and the religious College of St George. Edward gave land in the Lower Ward to the College including the Great Hall and chapel which was rededicated to St George (patron saint of England). The Order of the Garter remains the highest Order of Chivalry in the United Kingdom, the origin of its motto *Honi Soit Qui Mal Y Pense* (Shame on

Him Who Thinks Ill of It) being the subject of debate. Membership was limited to 26 Knights Companion, always including the Sovereign and the Prince of Wales, with the others being chosen by the Sovereign. Poor Knights (now called Military Knights) were also appointed to pray daily in the chapel on behalf of the Sovereign and the Companions in their absence. The major building works by surveyor William Wykeham included palatial new Royal apartments in the Upper Ward, a new gatehouse between the Upper and Lower Wards (now the Norman Gateway), accommodation for the Priest Vicars of the College of St George in the Lower Ward and a new tower (now the Mary Tudor Tower) to house the bells of the newly named St George's Chapel. Wykeham, who was later made Bishop of Winchester, also rebuilt the (now called) Winchester Tower on the north side of the Lower Ward.

Henry V (Lancaster) 1413-22 built in 1415 the Vicars Hall as a Common Hall for the Priest Vicars of the College of St George.

Edward IV (York) who became King in 1461 also made changes; his great achievement in 1475 was to begin building a new St George's Chapel on a much grander scale than its predecessor. It is one of the finest examples of English Perpendicular architecture and has similarities of style to Eton College chapel built from 1441 by its founder Henry VI (Lancaster) who was deposed by Edward. The Horseshoe Cloister was also begun at this time to provide new accommodation for the Priest Vicars of the College of St George. In 1479 the chapel bells were moved across from the (now called) Mary Tudor Tower to a new belfry in the (now called) Curfew Tower where they have remained ever since.

Henry VII (Tudor) 1485-1509 added the Henry VII tower to the Royal apartments and continued work on St George's Chapel.

Henry VIII (Tudor) 1509-47 built the new Main Gate which bears his name and finished St George's Chapel. He also created a wooden terrace along the outer north side of the Upper Ward, the forerunner of the North Terrace.

Mary I (Tudor) 1553-8 created new apartments in the Lower Ward for the Poor Knights of the Order of the Garter.

Elizabeth I (Tudor) 1558-1603 built the Elizabeth I Gallery in the Upper Ward and transformed her father's wooden (North) terrace into a stone structure. William Shakespeare wrote the comedy play *The Merry Wives of Windsor* which is said to have been first performed in the castle before the Queen.

The English Civil War resulted in the execution of **Charles I** (Stuart) in 1649 and the escape of his son Charles (II) to live in exile in France and Holland. The ensuing **Commonwealth Period** or **Interregnum** from 1649-1660 saw Windsor Castle used as a garrison for Parliamentary troops and a prison for Royalists while the structure of the castle and St George's Chapel suffered damage and theft. Windsor's Little Park and Great Park were sold off and the majority of the deer killed for food.

Charles II (Stuart) returned from exile in 1660 with a determination to repair damage, restore the property and land stolen during the Commonwealth period and to put his own stamp on the castle. Influenced by architectural styles he had seen while abroad he found the facilities at Windsor rather basic. From 1675-8 his architect Hugh May created the four storey Star Building on the north side of the Upper Ward to replace existing apartments. It bore a large Garter Star (an emblem of the Order) on the centre face and featured round headed windows (characteristic of May's work) which were also inserted into other buildings including the Henry III Tower. The North Terrace was widened at this time. Creation of The Long Walk in Windsor Great Park began from 1680 but did not extend as close to the castle as it does now. Charles had Burford House built just outside the castle for his mistress Nell Gwyn and her eldest son, Charles Beauclerk, who was made Earl of Burford and Duke of St Albans. The moat along the West End Wall of the castle was filled in (and houses later built close to the wall).

William III and Mary II (Stuart) joint rulers from 1689, preferred Hampton Court Palace but did spend some time at Windsor. With plans to build a formal garden, William purchased land to the north of the castle, extending the Little Park closer to the river and enclosing it with a brick wall. The public road from Windsor to Datchet ferry was re-routed along the edge of the river. In the town the Guildhall was completed in 1690.

Queen Anne (Stuart) 1702-14 enjoyed Windsor but preferred not to live in the castle and used a hunting lodge just south of the Upper Ward which later became known as the Queen's Lodge. In the Great Park, a carriageway along the Long Walk was created as well as Queen Anne's Ride. With a passion for hunting and horse racing Anne was responsible for the establishment of Ascot race course.

George III (Hanover) 1760-1820 was the next monarch to take a deep interest in Windsor encouraged by his wife Queen Charlotte; neither George I nor George II spent much time here and the castle had become run down. Initially King George and his family used the Queen's Lodge (which was enlarged) and Burford House (purchased from the cash-strapped 3rd Duke of St Albans) as summer residences in preference to living in the castle, the grounds of which were open for public use and recreation. Known as 'Farmer George' he encouraged the landscaping of the Great Park and the creation of farms. His architect James Wyatt made changes to the castle from 1800, the most obvious externally being the replacement of some of the round arched windows installed by Hugh May (for Charles II) with Gothic style pointed arches. In his later years the King suffered from bouts of illness (with physical and mental symptoms possibly indicating porphyria though this is not certain) which by 1810 had become so debilitating that he could no longer rule. His son George became Prince Regent from 1811 until 1820. As an architectural term, Regency loosely extends both before and after this time, up to the death of William IV. Many town buildings described in this book were either built or altered during the Georgian and Regency periods.

George IV (Hanover) 1820-30 was Regent for nine years but did not begin his considerable changes at Windsor until he became King. From 1824 architect Jeffry Wyatt began work on the Upper Ward. He was knighted in 1828 on the completion of the new Royal Apartments and changed his name to Sir Jeffry Wyatville to avoid confusion with his uncle James Wyatt. The external appearance of the Upper Ward was transformed with the heightening of towers, addition of battlements and machicolations, insertion of Gothic (pointed arch) windows and along the north front the new George IV, Cornwall and Brunswick Towers. On the south side the creation of the George IV Gateway (and new Lancaster Tower) saw the demolition of the Queen's Lodge and buildings in Park Street blocking the view of, and direct access to, the Long Walk. The most dramatic change was the transformation of the Round Tower by increasing its height by 30 feet (9 metres) and adding the Flag Turret. This produced the iconic shape by which the castle is best known today. The Lower Ward was left relatively untouched by these changes. In the Great Park the statue of George III (known as the Copper Horse) at the far end of the Long Walk was conceived by George IV in 1822 but not put in place on Snow Hill until 1831, a year after his death.

William IV (Hanover) 1830-37 was the brother of George IV. Wyatville continued with the work started in George IV's reign and designed the new Royal Mews to the south of the castle on land part occupied by Burford House. The work on this project extended beyond the death of Wyatville in 1840.

Queen Victoria (Hanover) 1837-1901 married Prince Albert of Saxe-Coburg & Gotha in 1840. No new major building programmes were undertaken during Victoria's reign but Albert was to have a significant influence on the town and castle restoration in the Lower Ward. Changes brought about under the Town Improvement Act 1848, in part instigated by Albert, removed slum housing and saw roads re-routed further away from the castle. These changes were partly funded by two rival railway companies who wanted to bring their rail lines into the town. The infamous George Street, a vice ridden slum, was replaced in 1849 by a railway station and by the 1850s all the buildings in Thames Street lining the West End Wall of the castle were demolished. When Wyatville died in 1840 his architect role was taken by Edward Blore whose work included restoration of the Salisbury Tower. Prince Albert replaced Blore with Anthony Salvin (and Sir George Gilbert Scott) who continued the restoration of the West End Wall. Prince Albert died in 1861 (after which Queen Victoria went into several years of deep mourning) but his work carried on. The most striking change was the enclosure of the bell chamber on top of the Curfew Tower within a distinctive French-style roof. The statue of Queen Victoria was erected to mark her Golden Jubilee in 1887 and the Great Western Railway station rebuilt to honour her Diamond Jubilee in 1897.

Little significant new building work (other than modernisation and repair) was carried out in the reign of subsequent monarchs until that of **HM Queen Elizabeth II** when in 1992 a serious fire broke out in the North-East corner of the Upper Ward. The fire started during restoration work and quickly spread, damaging many Royal apartments in varying degrees (some by fire and some by the water used to put it out) and destroying St George's Hall originally built by Edward III in 1362-5 for the Knights of the Garter. Many areas were restored to their former appearance but the opportunity was taken to carry out new work, such as a new ceiling for St George's Hall. What seemed a tragedy at the time, and indeed did destroy much important fabric, gave modern designers and craftsmen/women an opportunity to use their skills to create new structures within the castle, albeit at a great cost.

A note on dates

I have avoided the use of terms such as 18th century because for me (less numerate than some) it always involves a mini-calculation before working out that it means the 1700s. To avoid mini-calculations for others I have only used exact dates, decades or centuries – for example 1795, 1790s or 1700s depending on context or how precise is my knowledge of the date in question. Most dates are followed in brackets by a short, usually one word, label describing the Royal House or dynasty most appropriate to the date. There is some inconsistency in that, though the names of Royal Houses such as Plantagenet or Tudor are used, descriptions such as Georgian, Regency and Victorian are probably more useful and easily recognised by many than Hanover, the Royal House to which the monarchs of these three periods belonged.

There is, I hope, a reasonable enough correlation between the Royal labels and the architectural styles of the period to make their use worthwhile but of course styles do not come and go exactly in step with particular monarchs. For example the Regency covers the period from 1811-1820 when George III was too unwell to rule and his role was taken by his son George (later IV) who became Prince Regent. From an architectural point of view the term covers a wider timespan meaning that some (but not all) buildings from the late 1700s up to about 1840 might be categorised as Regency in style. My use of the labels is sometimes not strictly grammatical in that I have not always specified the noun to which these adjectives refer but hopefully this will be obvious when seen in context. For example the label Victorian might refer to a building or the Victorian period in general.

ROYAL HOUSES AND PERIODS REFERRED TO IN THE TEXT

Monarchs whose reign saw some significant input into Windsor Castle or the Royal Parks are listed in column 2 in bold text

NORMAN	**William I** 1066-1087	William II 1087-1100	
	Henry I 1100-1135	Stephen 1135-1154	
PLANTAGENET	**Henry II** 1154-1189	Richard I 1189-1199	John 1199-1216
	Henry III 1216-1272	Edward I 1272-1307	Edward II 1307-1327
	Edward III 1327-1377	Richard II 1377-1399	
LANCASTER		Henry IV 1399-1413	
	Henry V 1413-22	Henry VI 1422-1461 & 1470-1471	
YORK	**Edward IV** 1461-1470 & 1471-1483	Edward V 1483	Richard III 1483-1485
TUDOR	**Henry VII** 1485-1509		
	Henry VIII 1509-1547	Edward VI 1547-1553	
	Mary I 1553-1558		
	Elizabeth I 1558-1603		
STUART		James I 1603-1625	Charles I 1625-1649
		Commonwealth 1649-1660	
	Charles II 1660-1685	James II 1685-1688	
	William III 1689-1702	Mary II 1689-1694	
	Anne 1702-1714		
HANOVER (Georgian)		George I 1714-1727	George II 1727-1760
	George III 1760-1820		
HANOVER (Regency)	**George IV** 1820-1830 (Regency Period begins 1811; Prince George 'IV' becomes Prince Regent).		
	William IV 1830-1837		
HANOVER (Victorian)	**Victoria** 1837-1901		
SAXE-COBURG-GOTHA (Edwardian)		Edward VII 1901-1910	
WINDSOR		George V 1910-1936	Edward VIII 1936
		George VI 1936-1952	
	HM Elizabeth II 1952-		

The Maps

The numbers on the maps indicate the location of each view and the arrows show the position from which each view was drawn.

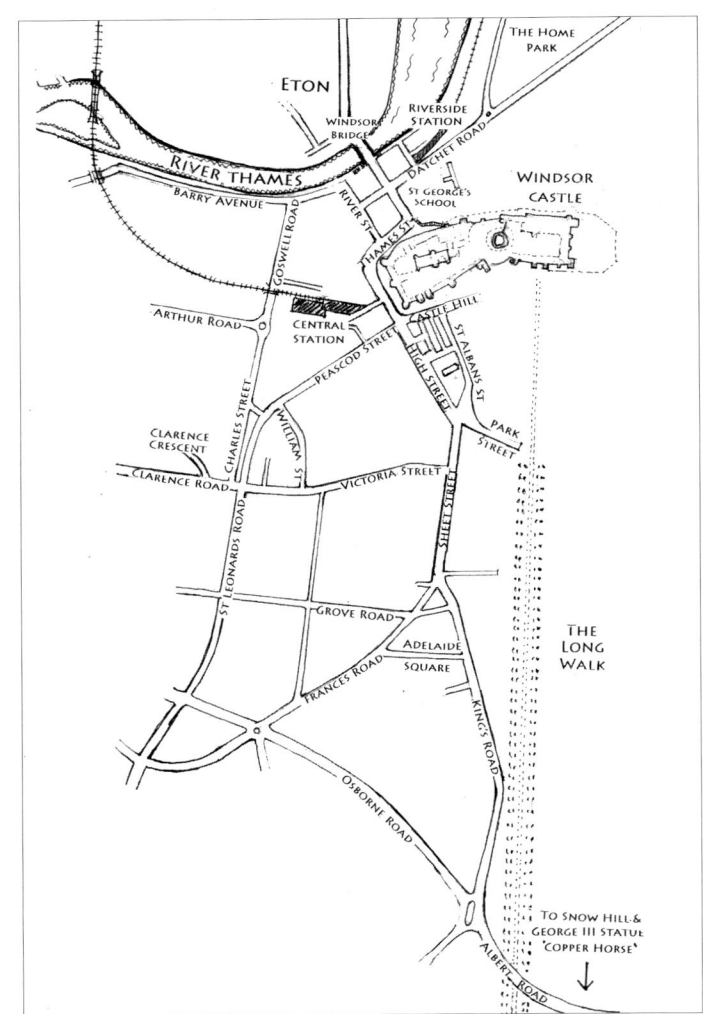

Map 1
Windsor Town – a general view

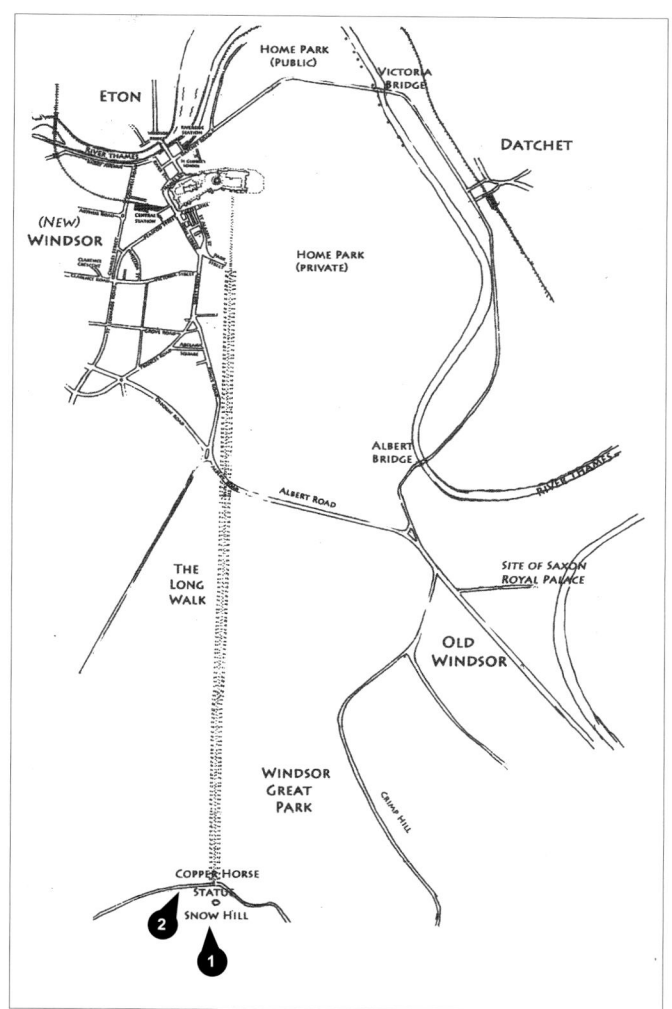

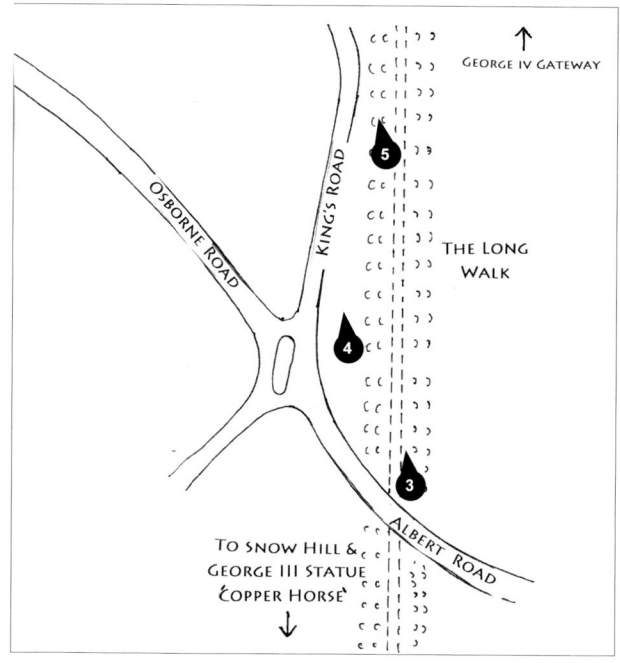

Map 3
Views 3–5

Map 2
Views 1–2

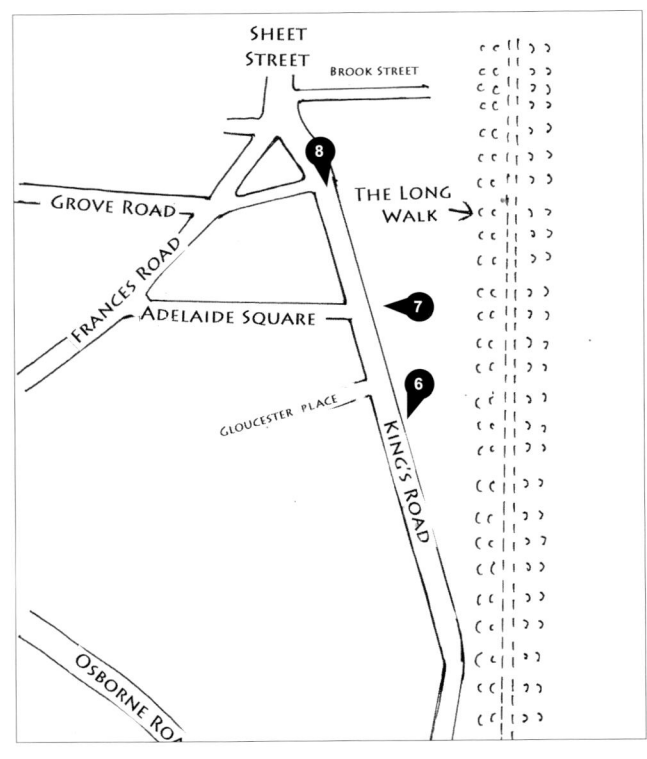

Map 4
Views 6–8

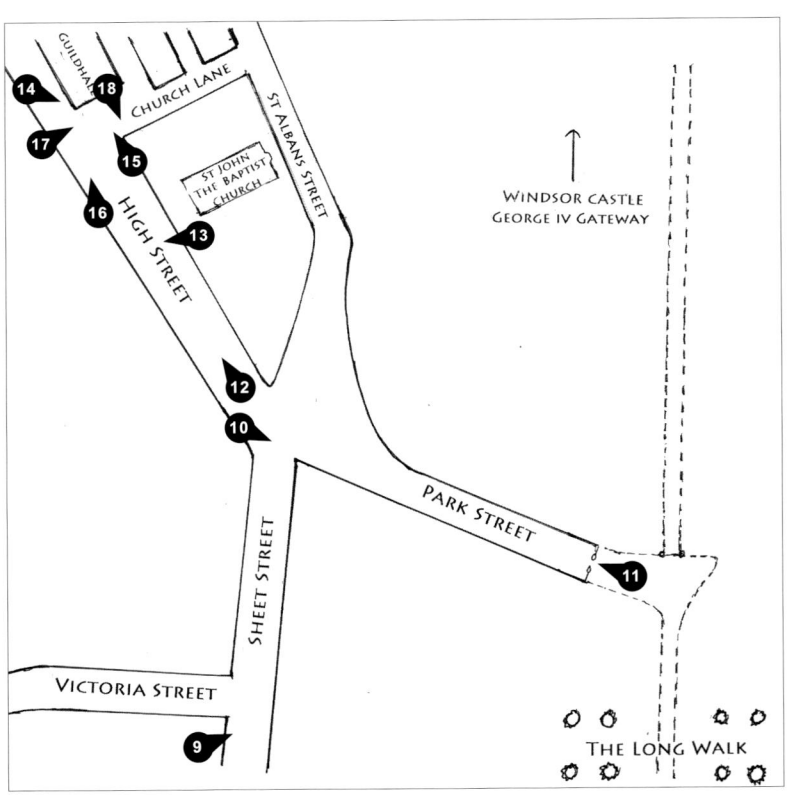

Map 5
Views 9–18

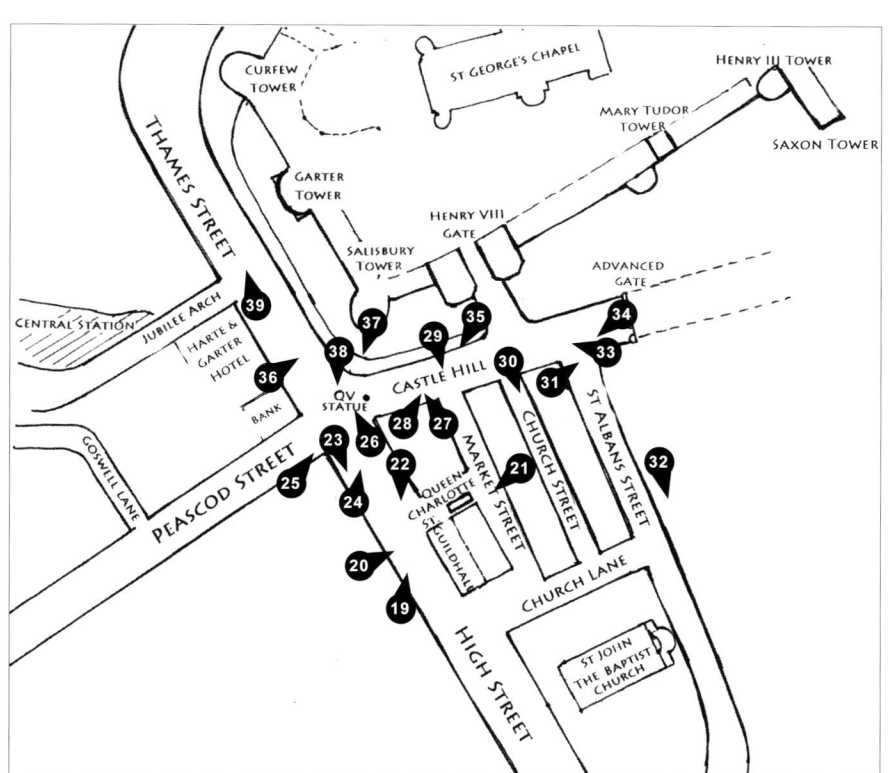

Map 6
Views 19–39

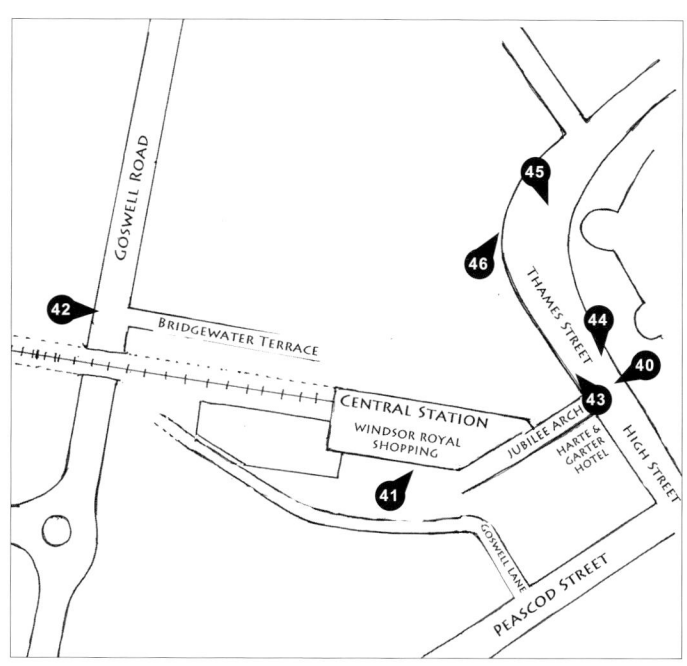

Map 7
Views 40–46

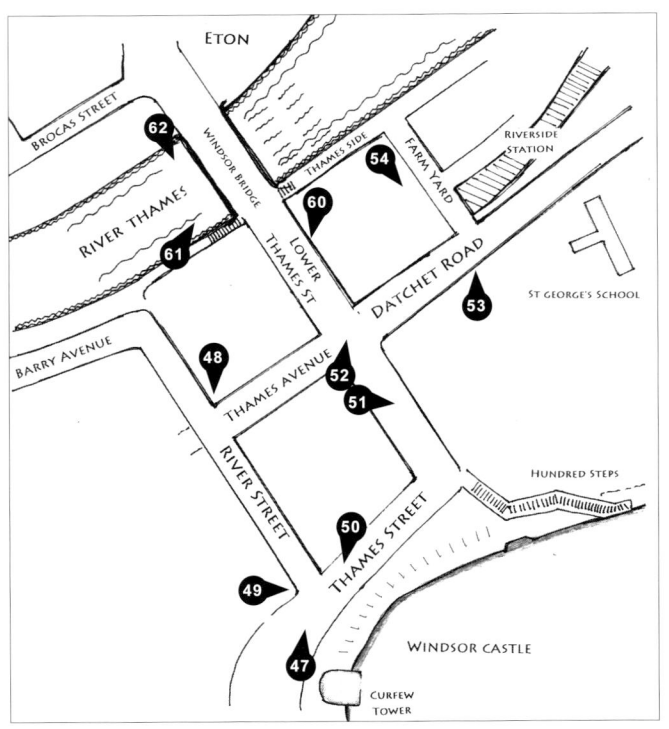

Map 8
Views 47–54 and 60–62

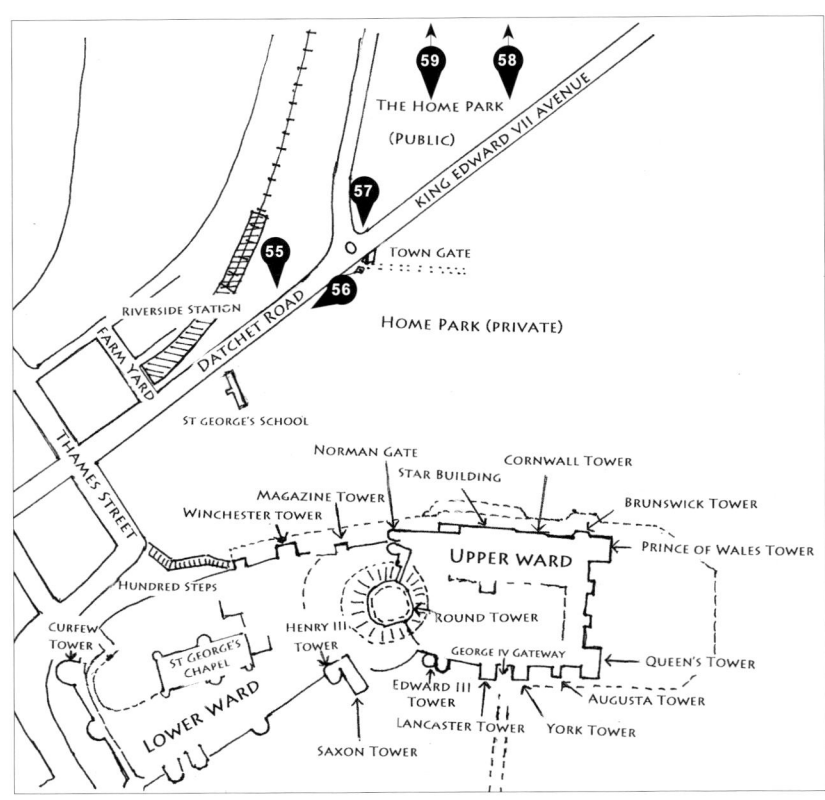

Map 9
Views 55–59

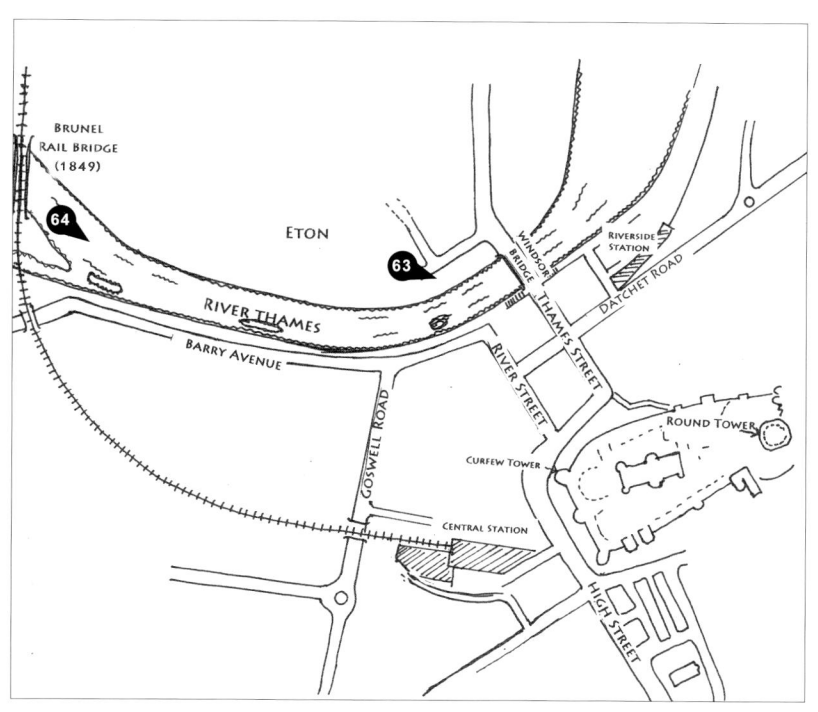

Map 10
Views 63–64

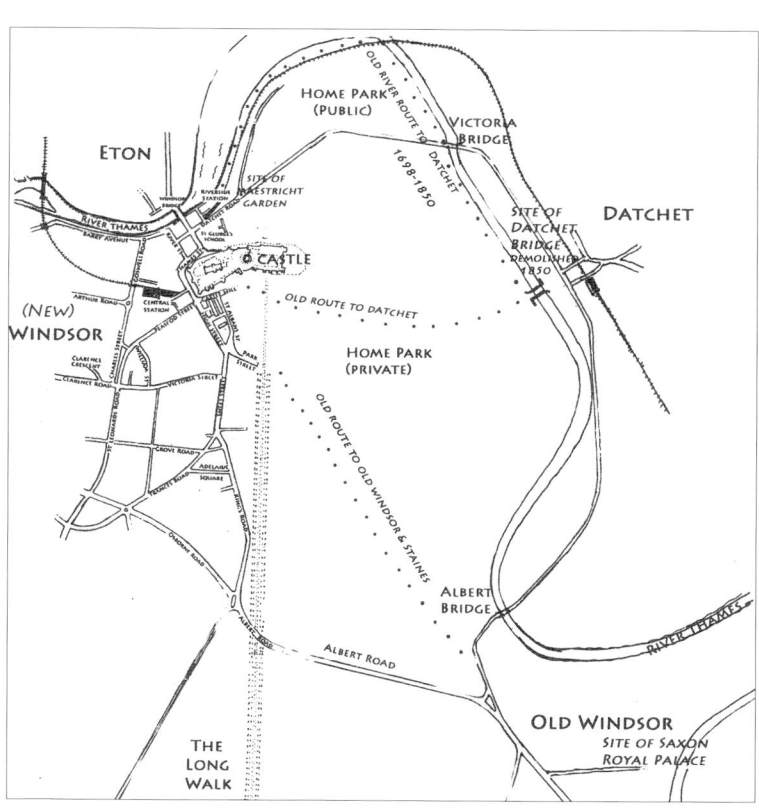

Map 11
The old routes

1 The Copper Horse on Snow Hill, Windsor Great Park

This is the view from the top of Snow Hill, one of the highest points in Windsor Great Park, showing the mounted statue of George III (known as **The Copper Horse**) and looking beyond towards the **Long Walk** and **Windsor Castle** in the distance. The statue, created for George IV to honour his father (though the two were not always on good terms), bears an inscription in Latin on the pedestal which reads 'Georgio Tertio Patri Optimo Georgius Rex' – 'George III Best of Fathers King George'.

Conceived by George IV in 1822, two years after his father's death, the 25 ton statue was created from 1824 –1828 by sculptor (Sir) Richard Westmacott (knighted 1837).

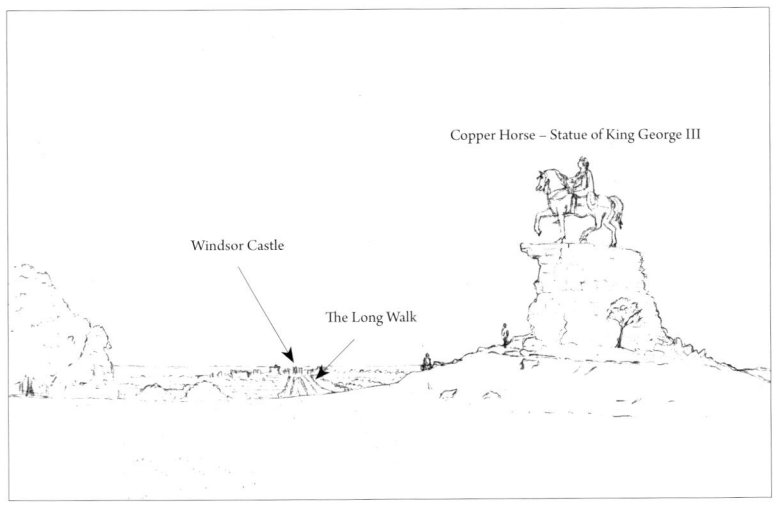

Copper Horse – Statue of King George III

Windsor Castle

The Long Walk

It is made from bronze, a copper alloy, (apparently derived from melted cannons) and has a green patina, a thin tarnish of coloured copper salts caused by reaction of the metal with chemicals in the atmosphere. It shows the King in classical Roman style wearing a laurel wreath, the lack of stirrups being intentional and not an oversight by the sculptor. Though the foundation stone was laid on George IV's birthday in 1829, construction of the granite base, overseen by his architect Sir Jeffry Wyatville, was delayed due to discussions on design and cost and not started until 1830. When the base was ready in 1831 the statue was transported from London to Windsor via Staines where a section of horse's leg was damaged and later needed re-casting. The unveiling took place on 24 October 1831 with no formal ceremony. George IV died in 1830 so never saw the statue in place.

The birds in the foreground are jackdaws, *Corvus monedula*, members of the crow family. Apparently they have been known to nest inside the horse statue, gaining access through a hole beneath the rider.

The view from Snow Hill is magnificent and well worth the visit, particularly on a clear day when visibility is good.

2 The Long Walk from Snow Hill, Windsor Great Park

This view, from the lower slope of Snow Hill, shows the **Long Walk** looking towards **Windsor Castle**. The avenue is located within Windsor Great Park, a large area of Crown Estate land including both farmed and landscaped areas, with a good proportion of the latter being open to the public. Creation of the Long Walk began in 1680 in the reign of Charles II (Stuart), probably by his architect Hugh May, and originally comprised a double row of trees on either side, all English elms *Ulmus procera*, totalling 1,625 in number. It was completed about 1696 (William III) and the central carriageway created for Queen Anne in 1710. At the Snow Hill end the tree rows originally carried on up the slope but in the 1800s these were cut down as they restricted the view towards the

castle. The tree-lined roadway extends from the Park Street Gate in Windsor *(View 11)* to the base of Snow Hill with a footpath continuing up to the statue. The distance from Park Street Gate to the Copper Horse is 2.5 miles (4 km).

Many of the original elms gradually succumbed to disease and from the 1920s plans were in hand to replace those worst affected. In the 1940s a programme of total replacement followed so that by 1946 felling and replanting was completed. Two different species were used – Horse Chestnut (*Aesculus hippocastanum*) on the inner rows and London Plane (*Platanus x acerifolia*) on the outer. During this process the distance between the outer rows was widened by 16 yards (15 m). In 1980 every other tree was removed to increase their spacing from 10 to 20 yards (9 to 18 m).

The deer shown in the picture roam freely in this part of the Great Park, which is fenced and designated as the Deer Park. Deer have been associated with the Park since at least the 1200s. Numbers were depleted heavily during the English Civil War (1640s) when they were killed for food, but they were re-introduced by Charles II following the restoration of the Monarchy in 1660. Both Fallow deer (*Dama dama*) and Red deer (*Cervus elaphus*) were present for much of this time but in 1941 (when more land was needed for wartime crops) the Fallow deer were removed and the Red deer reduced in number. In 1950 those remaining were transferred to other parks, so for nearly 30 years the Great Park had no deer until 1979 when Red deer, the larger species, were re-introduced from the Balmoral (Scotland) Estate of HM Queen Elizabeth II. This programme was overseen by the current Park Ranger, HRH Prince Philip, Duke of Edinburgh (husband of The Queen). The office of Park Ranger has existed since the 1600s and is always given to someone close to the Monarch, a trusted friend or a member of the Royal family.

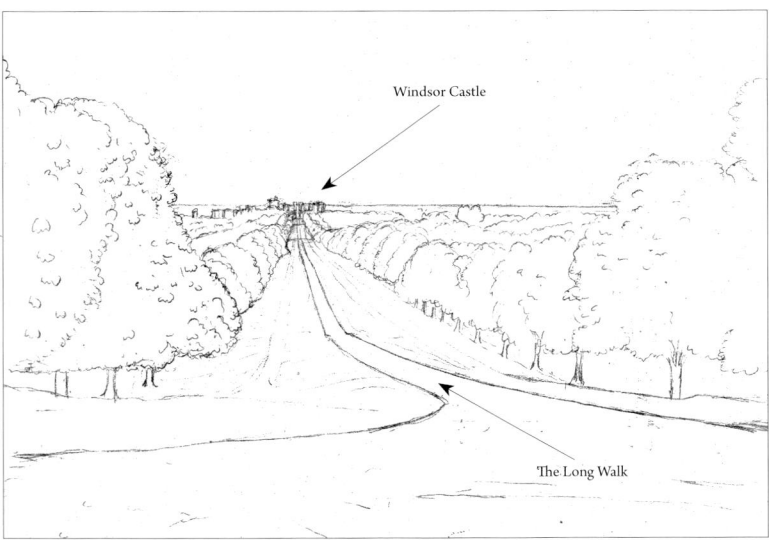

Windsor Castle

The Long Walk

3 The Long Walk from Albert Road

Albert Road (named after Prince Albert, the Consort of Queen Victoria) was created in 1850/51, one of the changes resulting from the Windsor Improvement Act 1848 which was finalised after a deal struck between the Crown and the London & South Western Railway. In return for permission to enter Windsor across Crown land north of the castle, the railway helped finance the replacement of old routes that led to Datchet and Old Windsor across the Home Park with new roads around its edge, thus affording the Royal household more privacy *(Map 11)*. Albert Road runs south east from Windsor towards Old Windsor and crosses the Long Walk slightly less than a mile (1.5 km) south of the castle.

The view towards the castle shows prominently the **Round Tower** on the mound and, to its right, the rounded **Edward III Tower** *(View 36)*. The Long Walk approaches the castle towards the **George IV Gateway** flanked by the square **Lancaster** (left) and **York** (right) **Towers**. The York Tower and the **Augusta Tower** have mediaeval origins but were heavily altered in the reign of George IV when the Lancaster tower was created, so forming a new and impressive gatehouse which remains the Sovereign's main entrance to the castle. This work was carried out by Sir Jeffry Wyatville, George IV's architect, who extensively remodelled parts of the castle in Gothic style from 1824 –1840. Buildings which blocked the view along the Long Walk from the proposed new castle gateway to Snow Hill (where the Copper Horse would later stand – *View 1*) were demolished. These included houses on the north side of Park Street *(Views 10 & 11)* and the Queen's Lodge, a building close to the South Front of the castle's Upper Ward which in the early 1700s had been a home/hunting lodge for Queen Anne and was later enlarged (1776/8) as a summer home for George III and Queen Charlotte.

The trees lining the Long Walk comprise Horse Chestnut (*Aesculus hippocastanum*) along the inner rows and London Plane (*Platanus x acerifolia*) on the outer. When they were planted to replace the original elms the plan was to see which grew better and perhaps remove one or the other species. As it turned out they have both grown well so each has been thinned out rather than one species culled. The London Plane is a tough species which grows well in many environments. The Horse Chestnut with its domed shape, early flowering and good autumn colour is very suitable for this location. However in recent years (since about 2007) the trees have been attacked by the Horse Chestnut leaf miner (*Cameraria ohridella*) a small moth whose larvae burrow through the leaves causing them to shrivel, turn brown by late summer and to fall early. The trees are not seriously harmed but the autumn colours of the Long Walk, which can be spectacular, have tended to be less splendid in recent years.

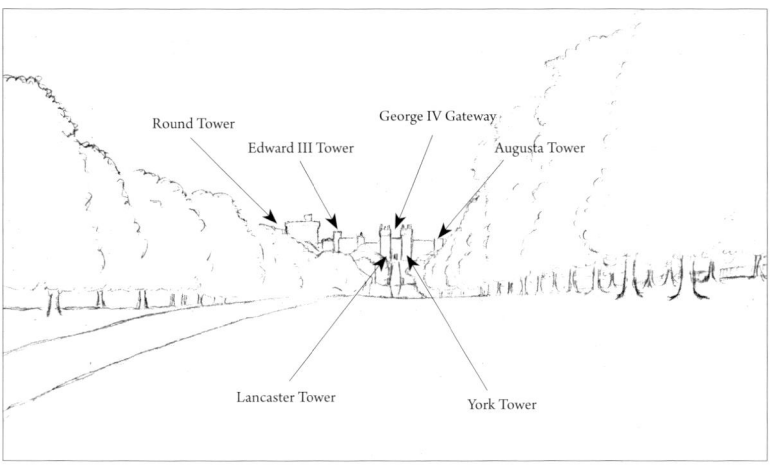

Round Tower
Edward III Tower
George IV Gateway
Augusta Tower
Lancaster Tower
York Tower

4 *Kings Road and Queen's Terrace*

Kings Road runs north towards Windsor town centre along the edge of the Long Walk. Once part of Sheet Street, the name first appeared in the early 1600s though apparently was not associated with any particular king.

On the right, London Plane (*Platanus x acerifolia*) form the outer rows of trees of the Long Walk and in the distance the **Round Tower** of the castle is visible. This picturesque area is much used by walkers (with or without dogs) and joggers.

The red brick building with sandstone dressings on the far left, partly hidden by trees, is **Hamilton Lodge**, built 1860/70 in Victorian Gothic (Revival) style. Gothic Revival architecture had its roots in the mid/late 1700s (Georgian), developing through the early 1800s (Regency) to reach its climax in the mid/late 1800s (Victorian). Its earlier

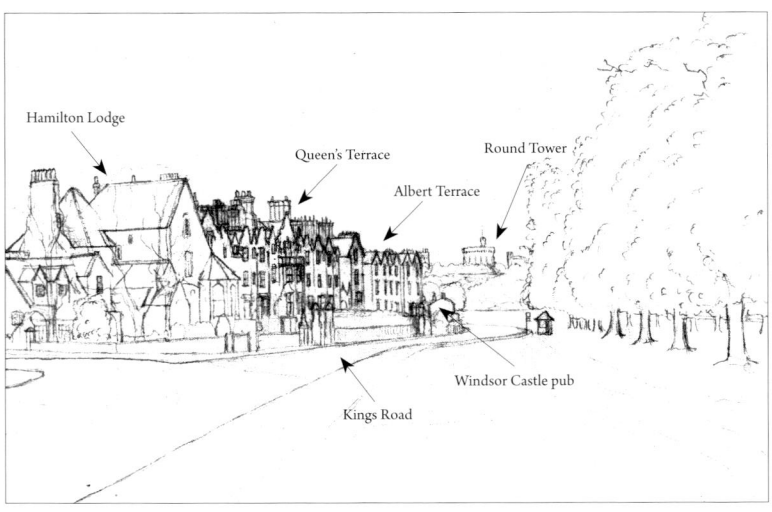

Hamilton Lodge

Queen's Terrace

Round Tower

Albert Terrace

Windsor Castle pub

Kings Road

years went hand in hand with a developing 'romantic' interest in the mediaeval period, including (often ruined) castles and abbeys, and copied elements from these buildings (rather than the classical Greek or Roman inspired influences found in traditional Georgian architecture). Characteristic is the use of the pointed arch for features such as window and door surrounds. At Windsor Castle, Gothic Revival elements were introduced by James Wyatt for George III around 1800 (*View 59*) and the style then went on to dominate the restructuring of the Upper Ward by Sir Jeffry Wyatville for George IV from 1824. Later in the century, the Victorian Gothic period saw many highly ornate buildings including churches, town halls, hotels, and railway stations with much decorated brickwork, surmounted by towers, pinnacles, large chimneys and steeply-pitched gabled roofs – an example being the Midland Hotel fronting St Pancras railway station in London, designed by (Sir) George Gilbert Scott.

Beyond is the large and highly ornamented **Queen's Terrace**. It dates from 1849 (Victorian) and is built in Jacobean style, copying features and ornaments found in mansions from the early 1600s (James 1 – Stuart) including the curved Dutch gable and finely patterned window glass. The work is typical of its architect, Samuel Teulon (1812-1873), who specialised in intricately decorated buildings, often in the Gothic revival style though he freely copied from any period of history. He favoured the use of polychrome (many coloured) brickwork which is shown in the red, blue/black and white bricks used in this terrace, including diamond and chevron patterns called diapering (*View 56*).

The simpler styled **Albert Terrace**, just beyond and directly adjoining, has a plaque dated 1845 (Victorian).

In the distance at the bend in the road is the **Windsor Castle pub** (*View 5*) and, opposite, a wooden bus shelter.

5 The Windsor Castle Pub, Kings Road and Round Tower

The **Windsor Castle public house** is situated further along Kings Road with a good view of Windsor Castle itself. It was a lodging house and beer retailer in 1846 (Victorian) and is now a public house.

As in the previous view, on the right hand side London Plane (*Platanus x acerifolia*) form the outer rows of trees of the Long Walk, their maple-like leaves visible in the foreground.

In the background is the **Round Tower**, the keep of the castle which has been

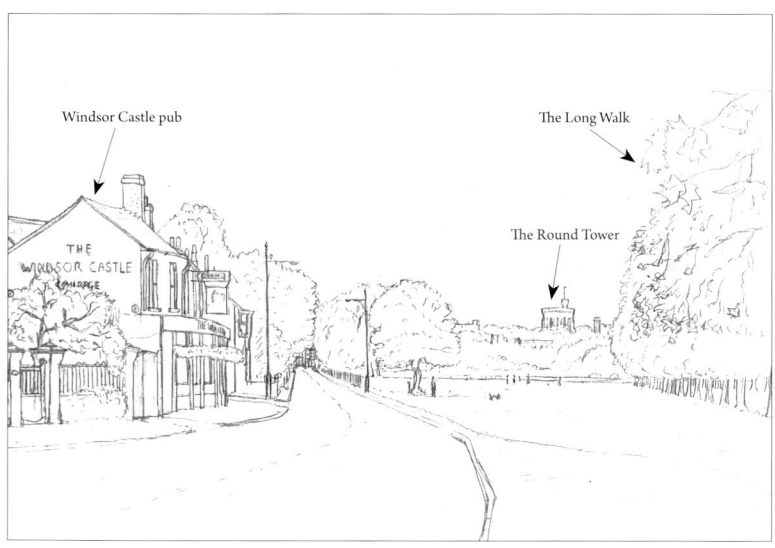

Windsor Castle pub

The Long Walk

The Round Tower

modified many times over centuries. The original wooden palisade or tower built in 1070 by William I (Norman) was converted to a circular stone structure by Henry II (Plantagenet) in 1170. Local flint and chalk was suitable for filling the centre of the thick walls but the outer faces required something stronger and more weather resistant. Heath stone, a very durable siliceous sandstone found at Bagshot some 10 miles (16 km) south of Windsor, proved an ideal material for the keep and many other parts of the castle. It was used in many subsequent building programmes though not always from the same source. The tower was rebuilt (not quite round) by Henry III (Plantagenet) in 1220 following subsidence of the mound and dramatically raised in height (1830) in the reign of George IV by his architect Sir Jeffry Wyatville *(See also View 31)*.

The castle started life as one of many, quickly built to secure newly won territory, but its good defensible position and location soon made it a favourite with Royalty, which it has remained ever since. Windsor is the oldest and largest continuously occupied castle in the world with modifications made to the structure, to a greater or lesser extent, in every century since it was founded. As the castle evolved from simple castle to fortress to palace some new works merely added to or altered the existing buildings; others obliterated what had gone before. This evolution is therefore complex and does require some effort to appreciate fully. As we continue the journey through the main thoroughfare of Windsor the structures of the castle will be shown as seen from the town streets and surrounding parkland in the order in which they appear (rather than a logical historical sequence). The brief historical notes accompanying the views will hopefully put the walls, towers and gateways from various periods of history into context as part of the whole castle.

6 Adelaide Terrace, Kings Road

This view of Kings Road looks back at **Adelaide Terrace** from the north, with the Windsor Castle public house just hidden around the bend in the road. Built in 1831 (Regency) it is named after the Queen Consort of William IV, Adelaide of Saxe-Meiningen, who gave her name to other buildings in this part of Windsor (and to the city of Adelaide in Australia). William IV succeeded his brother, George IV, in 1830 and died in 1837.

The terrace was among several properties built when, for the first time, land along Kings Road close to the Long Walk became available for development. The building is 16 bays* wide with a central four bay pediment (low triangular gable) beneath which

Adelaide Terrace

Nos. 54/56 Kings Rd

are four (Ionic) pilasters (flat representations of columns) and a balcony at 1st floor level. The walls at the front and sides are stuccoed (rendered with a smooth coating, in this case Roman cement). The building is typical of simpler-styled Regency architecture, shown by its elegant lines and some features influenced by Greek temple design. The central pediment is used to give the terrace (of individual dwellings) a passing resemblance to a large country house of the period.

Nos. 54/56 Kings Road, the building to the right of the terrace, only part of which is shown, was built in 1912 in the Arts & Crafts style. It had been designed in 1910 by architect Stephen Salter (1862-1956). Stephen's father (also Stephen) was a master boat builder who, with his brother John, built racing eights for Oxford when they defeated Cambridge in the University Boat Race for nine years in succession (1861-69). The firm later became Salters Steamers which still runs boats from Windsor and other Thames towns (*View 64*). Stephen Salter Junior decided not to join this business but to train as an architect. He became influenced by the Arts & Crafts movement which, broadly speaking, sought to return to more traditional craftsman-like methods of construction and design. An important influence on Stephen was the Arts & Crafts designer and architect Charles Voysey and some features on this house are typical of the latter's work including asymmetrical design, prominent cross gable, green tiles, a sloping buttress, mullioned and porthole windows and the use of a heart motif on some internal features. The house, originally called Amerden, was renamed Wistaria House by the present owners because of the Wistaria (a.k.a. Wisteria) growing around the house.

*A bay is the term used to describe a vertical division of a building as indicated by a feature such as a window, so 16 bays means 16 windows wide.

7 The Royal Adelaide Hotel

The blue-painted **Royal Adelaide Hotel**, built 1830/31, was named after the Queen Consort of William IV, Adelaide of Saxe-Meiningen. The hotel is late Regency classical with a stuccoed (smooth rendered) exterior, curved at the corners. Features include pilasters (flat pillar-like decorations) flanking the main door and the window to its right, a cornice and curved parapet at roof level and first floor French windows opening onto a cast iron balcony. One first floor window has a **balconette** (a French-window safety guard or false balcony sometimes called a Juliet balcony after Shakespeare's balcony scene in Romeo and Juliet). Decorated iron balconies became fashionable during this period, partly due to the increased availability and relative cheapness of iron. This went hand in hand with the fitting of French windows (effectively glazed doors) which likewise became popular.

Adelaide House, the white painted building on the left, is contemporary with and similar in style to the hotel.

The road between these two buildings, **Adelaide Square** was developed from 1833-1840. Any plans there might have been to continue on to create a proper Square never materialised, but the name remained.

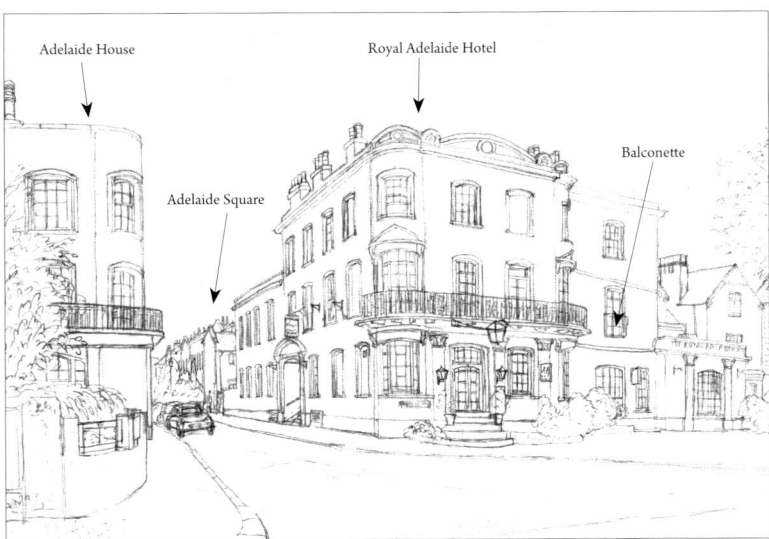

8 *Brunswick Terrace, Nos. 39–63 Kings Road*

This terrace of 13 houses built probably in the 1820s shows many typical Regency features. Most characteristic are the first floor **French windows** opening onto **cast-iron balconies** with wood-lattice **verandas** topped by Chinese-influenced pagoda style roofs. Built of yellow London stock brick, it is one of several up-market terraces and houses created about this time when land close to the Long Walk became available for development. The terrace is named after (Queen) Caroline of Brunswick, the wife of George IV, with whom he had a difficult relationship both as Prince of Wales and King (from 1820). She is described as an unconventional person, lacking qualities generally regarded as attractive and with dubious personal hygiene, though for a short while before her death in 1821 she was more popular with the masses than the King. Perhaps they did not get that close to her. It seems the Prince married for money and lived to regret it.

The houses have mostly kept their original features including the **sash*** windows and railings. Each is of three storeys and basement with steps (and typically railings) up to the front door, which has a semi-circular fanlight above. All except three have retained their roofed verandas.

No. 63 was the home of A. Y. Nutt, Artist and Architect (and Surveyor to the Dean and Canons of St George's), announced by a Blue Plaque.

The smaller terraces at each end are contemporary with the main block.

* The sash window, in which window panels called sashes slide up and down vertically using cords and counterweights, was invented in England in the 1600s and became very popular during the 1700s (Georgian). Up to this point casement windows were the standard with window panels opening on side hinges. French windows, which are effectively glazed doors, still required hinges. During the Georgian period, modernisation of older buildings usually involved replacement of casements by sashes.

French window

Iron balcony

Veranda

Sash window

9 *Hadleigh House, Sheet Street*

Hadleigh House, facing the junction of Sheet Street and Victoria Street, is regarded as one of the finest Georgian buildings in Windsor. The main house and the smaller buildings either side (wings) were built together as a unit in 1795 for William Thomas, who became Mayor of Windsor in 1805. He was an apothecary (the forerunner of a pharmacist) and later, a surgeon. The next occupant was John O'Reilly, a surgeon apothecary to the Royal households of George IV and William IV, followed by another medical man, Henry Brown who used the building on the left (north wing) as his surgery. A subsequent owner in the 1900s named this building Clifford Lodge.

The main building, **Hadleigh House**, has five bays with three main storeys (plus an attic and a basement) with taller windows (and higher ceilings) on the ground and first floors. It demonstrates the typical Georgian symmetry and proportion known as Palladian style, based on the work of Italian architect Andrea Palladio (1508-80) who himself drew inspiration from classical Roman architecture.

The **mansard roof*** with dormer windows (developed in France and popularised by Francois Mansart in the 1600s) was brought to Britain in this late Georgian/Regency period, the shallow-pitched top section and steep sides allowing more space for (servants') accommodation to be fitted in. The increased availability of light (Welsh) slates, rather than heavy clay tiles, helped make this shape of roof easier to construct. There is a large chimney at each end. Unusually for a building of this size, it is only one room deep with windows at the rear facing out on to the Long Walk. The upper windows on the centre and outer bays are flanked by Venetian shutters whilst on the ground floor all windows have blind boxes, originally housing external blinds which could be pulled down to keep out the sun. The doorway has a (triangular) pediment above, supported by Ionic columns and an ornate fanlight (to let light into the hallway). The brick wall to the front has a gateway with fine wrought iron gates and lamp holders on the pillars, all original features.

*Technically the mansard roof has four pitched sides while this roof, with two pitched sides (front and back) between brick end walls, is a gambrel roof. It is however described as a mansard roof in English Heritage records.

Mansard roof

Blind box

10 *Park Street*

Park Street was once the starting point for an important route from Windsor to London (via Frogmore, Old Windsor and Staines) and sometimes favoured during the horse-drawn coaching era because it avoided the steep climb up from Windsor Bridge to the town centre *(Map 11)*. It was truncated about 1824 when properties at the far end on the left (beyond the present gate) were demolished as part of a plan by Sir Jeffry Wyatville (George IV's architect) to create a new approach from the Long Walk towards the castle. Further changes in 1850/51 saw the route via Frogmore blocked when, following the coming of the railways, Albert Road was built to carry it further south and away from the Home Park *(View 3)*. Park Street Gate *(View 11)* now marks the end of the street

and its boundary with the Long Walk. The street has changed name over the centuries; originally called Moor Street (because it crossed Frog Moor), then Cuthorse Well Street, later Pound Street (an animal pound was located here) and finally Park Street in 1742.

This view is from the end of the High Street just before its junction with Sheet Street. A more apt name in recent times might be Car Park Street as it is extremely rare to see it devoid of parked cars, as in the picture; this only being possible on the day of a State Visit (with its ceremonial military parade through the town) when all vehicle parking is banned. The Street is noted for its high proportion of Georgian buildings, though on the north side, more visible here, some of them are tastefully designed replacements dating from the 1900s.

An old coaching inn, the New Inn (Hotel), once stood at the centre-left foreground of the picture but was demolished in 1931. The large Georgian building on the left **No. 20** dates from late 1700s, the pair of taller buildings further down **Nos. 23 & 24** from 1739 but the smaller dwellings with dormer windows filling the gaps are younger (1910). Towards the far end on this side is the **Two Brewers** public house with a long history and a frontage from the late 1700s. Beyond, bordering the Long Walk, is **Cambridge Lodge** *(View 11)*.

Nos. 12-16 the stuccoed (rendered) curved-corner terrace on the right, built in 1830 (Regency), has been likened in style to buildings in London's Regent St by architect John Nash. Set back from the main face on the north side of the building are two pairs of very large Composite columns (known as giant columns because they extend over two storeys).

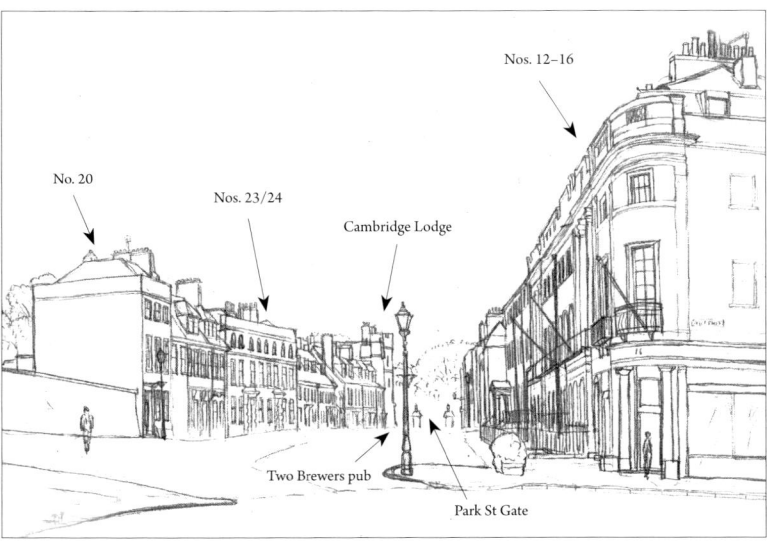

No. 20

Nos. 23/24

Cambridge Lodge

Nos. 12–16

Two Brewers pub

Park St Gate

11 Park Street Gate

Standing close to Park Street Gate we look back along Park Street towards its junction with High Street, Sheet Street and St Albans Street.

Park Street Gate has two octagonal pillars topped by lamps. Built during the 1820s (Regency) by Sir Jeffry Wyatville as part of the rebuilding programme for George IV, it is similar in style to the Advanced Gate in Castle Hill *(View 31)*. Buildings behind and to the right of this view had been demolished earlier in the 1820s to clear the vista from the new George IV Gateway to the Long Walk *(View 3)*. The castellated Cambridge Lodge (not seen but to the right of the picture) and the Cambridge Gate were added to guard the boundary between the Long Walk and the castle grounds.

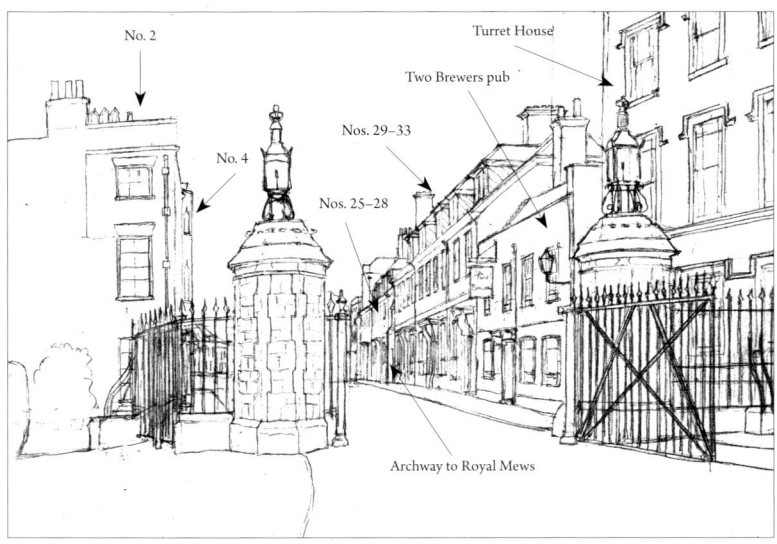

On the far right is the lower part of **Turret House** with an early 1800s (Regency) frontage, topped by a gable. The façade, which may hide an earlier building, is built of white brick much of it stuccoed (rendered). The sash windows have drip moulds above. To its left The **Two Brewers** public house is similarly older than its yellow brick late 1700s (Georgian) front would suggest. It is said to have been a coffee house (popular in the later 1600s/1700s) before becoming a pub. To reveal its appearance better some of its usual covering of window boxes and hanging baskets has been omitted from the picture. Beyond, Nos. **29-33** is a row of more modern housing with hipped dormers from about 1910 designed in neo Georgian style to blend in. Next, a buttress marks the position of the **Archway to the Royal Mews** located behind Park Street *(View 32)*. This was built by Edward Blore, successor to Wyatville in the 1840s (Victorian). Further on is another row of 1900s houses **Nos. 25-28**. The rest of this side of the street is better seen in *View 10*.

No. 2 the red brick building on the far left with rendered parapet and side wall dates from the 1700s (Georgian). The ogee arched window of **No. 4** (also Georgian) is part of a projecting oriel (upper floor bay) window above an old coaching entrance to Black Horse Yard to the rear of the building. The Black Horse, a former coaching inn, was located here. It is said that in Victorian times, after the inn had closed, the area behind was used by local butcher John Bedborough for keeping pigs and as a slaughter house, causing complaints from neighbours. During the late 1800s/early 1900s (Victorian/Edwardian) Bedborough ran a butcher's shop from No. 1 Castle Hill *(View 25)*.

12 *High Street, looking north with Castle Guard and Band*

This view shows the High Street looking north towards the Guildhall.

The band of the Grenadier Guards leads a contingent of Coldstream Guards (the Old Guard) back to Victoria Barracks in Sheet Street following the Changing of the Guard ceremony at the castle. Leading the band, carrying a mace, is the Drum Major. There are five Foot Regiments in the Household Division of the British Army – Grenadier, Coldstream, Scots, Irish and Welsh Guards and one Mounted Regiment, the Household Cavalry Regiment formed in 1992 from the Life Guards and the Blues and Royals. Bands from any of these (or other military Regiments) may accompany the guard which is often (though not always) provided by the Foot Guard Battalion currently stationed at Victoria Barracks. The guard change takes place every day in mid-summer and on alternate days during the rest of the year (but never on Sunday).

On the left, **No. 7 High Street** with the projecting oriel (upper floor bay) window dates from the late 1700s (Georgian) with the front altered in the 1800s (Victorian). **Nos. 8 and 9** further on are also late Georgian, the latter being set well back from the road with only a ground floor modern shop front on the street. The building in the right foreground, built in 1886, was originally the **London & County Bank** (later Westminster, then NatWest) and is now an office. The gabled Union Hotel, demolished in the early 1900s, once stood just beyond, adjoining the bank. The tower of the **Parish Church** (*View 14*) is seen above the trees.

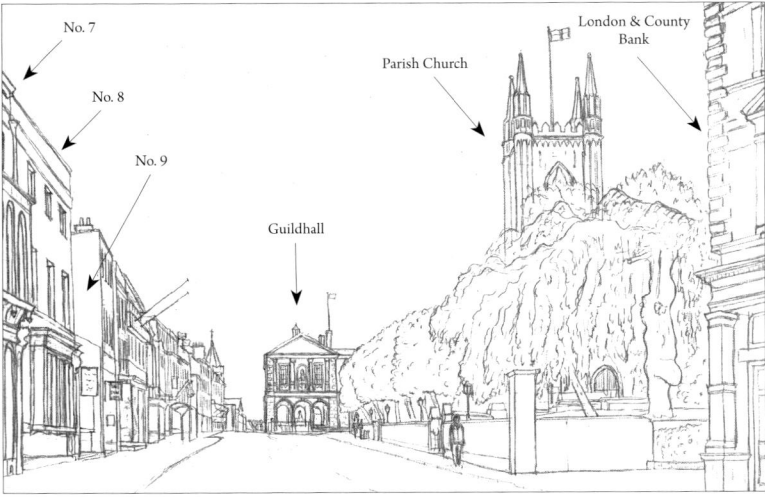

No. 7

No. 8

No. 9

Guildhall

Parish Church

London & County Bank

43

13 *Castle Hotel with Coldstream Guards' Band*

Further up the High Street we look across from the churchyard wall to the Castle Hotel with a ceremonial (Old) Guard returning from the castle to Victoria Barracks, this time accompanied by the band of the Coldstream Guards. All five of the Foot Guard Regiments wear similar ceremonial uniforms with red tunics and bearskin caps, each being distinguished by details such as the grouping of buttons, collar badges and the plume (or hackle) in the bearskin. The Coldstream Guards have their tunic buttons in twos, a red plume on the right side of the cap and a Garter Star on the collar.

The Castle Hotel (No. 18 High Street) in its present form dates from around 1800 (late Georgian/Regency), with later alterations. There have been inns on this site since mediaeval times one of which, The Bell, merged in the 1700s with the Mermaid

next door to become the Bell and Castle. This was renamed The Castle in 1809. The building, faced with stucco (smooth render), was originally 11 bays (windows) wide with the six bay section (now the central part) slightly projecting and with an access passage for horse-drawn coaches and later, cars. The five bay left-hand section has a different history. Here stood, until the 1920s, a four storey (probably Georgian) building with shops on the ground floor. This was acquired by the Castle then demolished and replaced by a single storey structure, probably for a newly located garage access, at about the time of a change of ownership from the Home Counties Public Houses Trust Ltd to Trust Houses Ltd. This, in turn, was replaced after WWII (late 1940s/early 1950s) by the present Regency-style section (with garage access) so that the hotel now appears more or less symmetrical. The iron balcony has an anthemion and scroll design, popular in the Regency period.

The building to the left of the hotel, **Nos. 15-17 High Street**, is mid/late 1700s (Georgian) though evidence of 1500s (Tudor) timbers was found within No. 17 during alterations in the mid-1900s. Nos. 15/16 form the section with dormers and clay-tiled roof while No. 17 was altered in the early 1800s to give it a more fashionable appearance by removing the old roof, building up the front wall, then adding a parapet and a shallower slate roof. This well illustrates how buildings of this type were altered in the Georgian/Regency period.

14 *St John the Baptist Church and No. 52 High Street*

The Parish Church of Windsor, St John the Baptist, dates from 1822 (Regency) when it replaced a mediaeval church (1100s) which had fallen into disrepair. It was thought better to rebuild than to renovate. The architect was Charles Hollis (*View 61*), a relative unknown at the time, though the work was overseen by a better known figure, Jeffry Wyatt (who on being knighted by George IV in 1828 changed his name to Sir Jeffry Wyatville) and built by James Bedborough (*View 17*) and Richard Tebbot. It is a fairly plain-styled Gothic revival building (using pointed arches) faced with ashlar (smooth faced, tightly jointed) blocks of Bath stone and is notable internally for the cast iron columns and ribs which support the roof. Three of the eight bells (from 1711) were transferred from the old church, the remainder being recast in 1822 at Whitechapel Bell Foundry. The tower has a clock to the front and on the left side (as viewed) a circular panel with the Windsor Coat of Arms. At the rear of the church is a chancel and apse added in 1870 by Samuel Teulon (*Views 4 & 32*).

The building to its left, **No. 52 High Street**, has proved difficult to research as it is not described in any books relating to Windsor history. It dates from at least the 1700s (Stuart/Georgian), possibly earlier, and was altered in the 1800s. In a painting from 1830 it is shown with dormers and very small bays to the front but no other adornments.. It seems likely that the fancy Gothick* style woodwork (window architraves with finials** and a cusped cornice along the eaves) and the larger bays at the front were added about 1840 (late Regency/early Victorian). The property is marked as an inn/public house (with bays) on maps from 1860 and 1868. The 1861 census records that John Clode (a wine merchant and Mayor of Windsor in 1854) lived here with his wife Sarah and may have managed the establishment. Local directories show it occupied by Ind Coope brewers in 1890 (listed as wine merchants) and a large advertising lamp suspended over the door on an 1895 photograph reads Ind Coope Wine Shop (or Beer Shop?). In the same photo there are signs that a florist was using the left hand ground floor. There were others sharing in this period (Tax Office, Insurance Agent) and by 1904 Giddy & Giddy (Auctioneers, Valuers and later, Estate Agents). In 1909 Ind Coope left and opened a beer shop in Peascod Street while Giddy & Giddy became the sole occupiers. The building has been an Estate Agents premises ever since, currently Hamptons.

The anthemion and scroll detail of the **Castle Hotel** balcony is shown on the far right.

*Gothick is a fancier Regency version of Gothic.
**Finial – small adornment or finishing piece to part of a building or furniture – these being shaped like onion domes.

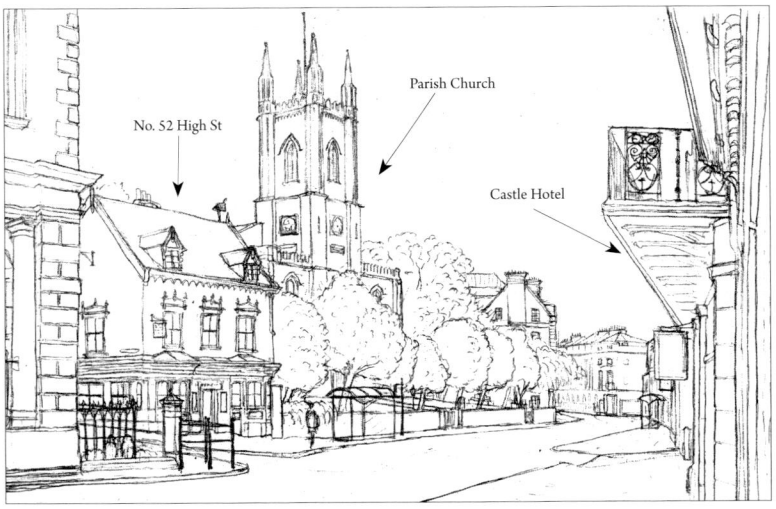

No. 52 High St

Parish Church

Castle Hotel

47

15 Guildhall (and Castle Hotel and Caleys) from No. 52 High Street

This view shows the **Guildhall** from the south with the bays of **No. 52 High Street** in the foreground and the **Castle Hotel** and **Caleys** opposite (*View 22*).

The **Guildhall** was completed in 1690 in the reign of William III (Stuart). It replaced the Market House, a wooden structure from 1592 (Tudor) located close to the present site and demolished in 1687 due to its dilapidated condition. The new building was originally planned as the Market House but, because almost from the outset council meetings and courts were held in the chamber above the open corn market, it very soon became the Guildhall.

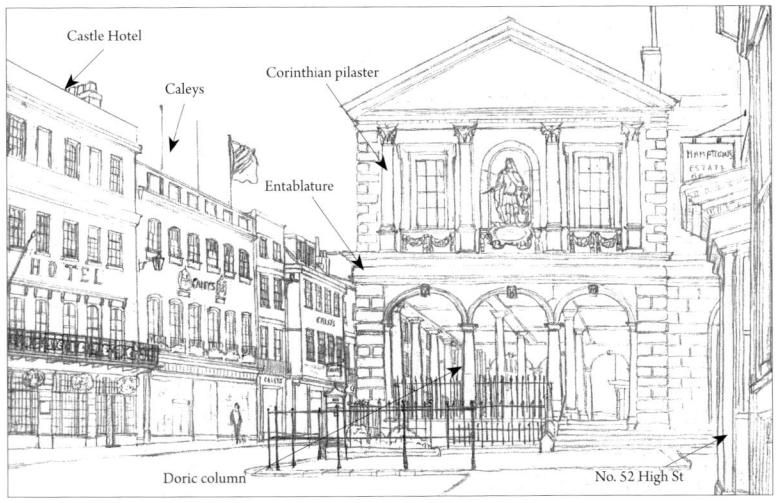

The building was designed by (Sir) Thomas Fitch (or Fitz), Surveyor of the Cinque Ports, but he died in 1689 a few days after being knighted and a year before the building work was completed. It is often said that Sir Christopher Wren was then asked to oversee the project but there is apparently no evidence that he was required because a skilled master mason from Windsor Castle, John Clark, was in charge of the day to day work. This led to another oft repeated but probably untrue tale that the four pillars in the centre of the building, which at first glance seem to be supports, were added by Sir Christopher Wren in 1690 on the orders of the Corporation whose members doubted that the design was safe without them. Though appearing to comply, he left a small gap between the pillars and the ceiling so that they offered no structural support. The more likely explanation for the central pillars being where they are is explained in the latest Guildhall guide (2011). Originally the building was symmetrical with five pillars (Doric columns) on each long side (east and west) and two on each short side (north and south). When an extension was added in 1829/30 (*View 16*) the five pillars on the east side became redundant and were removed. It was at this time that the councillors suggested that four of these be used as extra support during the building work. Possibly the extension architect, James Bedborough, left the gaps though another suggestion is that the weight of the new extension slightly distorted the older part and pulled the ceiling away from the pillars.

The south side, seen here, shows three arches and Roman-style **Doric columns** on the ground floor supporting an **entablature** (the horizontal multi-layered stone section inspired by Classical temple design). Above this, the first floor has **Corinthian pilasters** (flat pillars), large windows and a niche in which resides a **statue of Prince George of Denmark** (husband of Queen Anne) added in 1713 by the son of Sir Christopher Wren, also Christopher, a Member of Parliament for Windsor. At the opposite end of the building a statue of Queen Anne (who became Queen in 1702) had been added in 1707.

16 *Guildhall from Castle Hotel with Blues & Royals Band*

Here the Guildhall is seen from the other side of the street, with the Blues & Royals band returning with the (Old) Guard to Victoria Barracks. The Blues & Royals, once a separate Regiment, was merged in 1992 with another Regiment, the Life Guards, to form the Household Cavalry Regiment (one of the six Regiments of the Household Division) though both retain their distinctive uniforms. Simply put, the Blues & Royals wear blue tunics and a red plume on their metal helmets while Life Guards wear red tunics with a white helmet plume. The Band members are seen here in their winter cloaks. Foot Guards, with bearskin caps, wear grey greatcoats during the colder months.

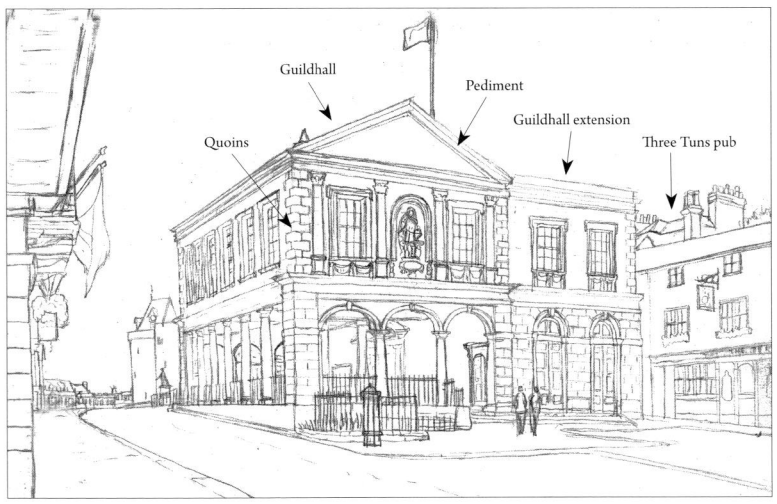

The form of the **Guildhall**, as completed in 1690 (William III – Stuart), is more clearly seen. The five side-pillars (plus half-pillars at the corners), and the three arches with pillars are all made from Portland Stone. The upper section has six windows on the western side and at each end two windows and a niche. The southern niche (seen here) houses the statue of Prince George of Denmark (husband of Queen Anne) dressed in Roman military uniform. The white stones finishing off the corners are called **quoins**. Above is the large (triangular) **pediment**. The quoins and window surrounds, made from Bath Stone, developed cracks and were replaced in 1970 during a refurbishment.

The **Guildhall extension** was added in 1830 (Regency). It was designed and built by James Bedborough, an experienced builder/stone mason and principal contractor to Sir Jeffry Wyatville who remodelled substantial sections of Windsor Castle for George IV. In particular he was employed to raise the Round Tower to its current height. Bedborough, who was elected Mayor in 1846 and 1853, had already built the new Parish Church in 1822 (with Richard Tebbot) *(View 14)*. Before the extension building could commence a number of buildings close by were purchased and demolished. It is perhaps shocking that in 1851 the main Guildhall building (now Grade 1 listed) became in such need of repair that there were calls for its demolition.

The Guildhall was used for council meetings and as a courtroom from 1690 until 1974 when local government changes made most of these uses redundant. Since 1998 the building has been licensed for wedding ceremonies. In April 2005 HRH Prince Charles and Mrs Camilla Parker-Bowles (now Duchess of Cornwall) were married here and a few months later came the civil partnership ceremony for Elton John and David Furnish. In 2011 a new Windsor and Royal Borough Museum opened in the ground floor of the extension.

Just behind the Guildhall extension is the Three Tuns public house *(View 17)* and further along the High Street the castle walls are visible.

51

17 Church Lane and The Three Tuns from Castle Hotel

The south face of the **Guildhall** is shown again and from this angle the door to the Mayor's entrance can be seen behind the pillars. Large vaults (basements) were dug in 1686 before building work started and initially used for storage. A large part of this underground area was much later converted into public toilets. A **Victorian green post box** stands close by. The hexagonal Penfold pillar box was the design used between 1866 and 1879. At first all were painted green until red was introduced as the standard colour from 1874.

The Three Tuns public house has an important history. It was built in 1518 (Tudor)

Nos. 8/9 Church St
Three Tuns pub
Royal Free School
Ship Inn
Victorian postbox
No. 4 Church Lane

as a meeting house or Guild Hall for the Fraternity of the Holy Trinity or Trinity Guild. It was a merchants' guild (with some religious element) but any role it might have had in local government or as a precursor of the local Council/Corporation (as is sometimes stated) seems unclear. From the 1600s (Stuart) it was also an inn, but still used for meetings. Though elements of the original building (including beams) still exist within, the facade (external features) visible today dates mainly from the early 1800s (Regency) or later.

Church Lane is one of the ancient streets of the market area that runs along the edge of the churchyard up to St Albans Street (formerly Priest Street). The gabled building **No. 4** apparently dates from 1423 (Henry VI) and to its right is an arched passage known as the **Engine House**, where the Windsor Fire Engine was kept from 1803. Next door is a public house which has had many name changes; once **The Ship Inn**, it is currently known as the Blarney Stone. It dates from the late 1700s/early 1800s (Georgian/Regency), and is faced with stucco (render) which is rusticated (deeply grooved to simulate stone work). The red brick building at the far end on the right is the former **Royal Free School** built in 1725/6 (Georgian) (*View 32*). **Nos. 8/9 Church Street**, the gabled corner building on the left, is of interest. Built around 1500 (Tudor) it has two gables and a jetty (overhang) facing Church Lane and an early 1700s (Georgian) frontage on Church Street. From 1818, it became the **Windsor General Dispensary** which offered free medical treatment for the poor, including smallpox vaccinations. One of the first patrons was Queen Charlotte (wife of George III), followed by George IV in 1821 who allowed it to be named the Windsor Royal General Dispensary.

No. 52 High Street on the right of the picture is described in *View 14*.

18 *High Street from the Guildhall with Grenadier Guards and Blues & Royals Band*

This view looks back down the High Street from just inside the open area of the Guildhall. The Old Guard returns from the castle to Victoria Barracks. Grenadier Guards wear a white plume on the left hand side of the bearskin cap (barely visible at this angle), single spaced buttons and a 'grenade fired proper' emblem on the collar. The Blues & Royals band is ahead of the Guard in the distance wearing normal (summer) uniform rather than the cloaks seen in winter. They wear blue tunics and metal helmets with a red plume.

In the left foreground is **No. 52 High Street**, now an Estate Agent but with a varied

use over the years as described in *View 14*. The white painted stuccoed (rendered) building dates to at least the 1700s (Stuart/Georgian), perhaps earlier, with the fancy ornamentations and bays added in the mid 1800s (Regency/Victorian). Behind, the Parish Church tower flies the St George's flag.

On the right, in the foreground we start with the **Castle Hotel** extension and **Nos. 15-17 High Street** as described in *View 13*. Next door **No. 14** is late 1700s (Georgian) and once used as a Vicarage. **No. 13** is of particular interest due to its very large first floor windows. The front part at least was built around 1840 (Victorian) and by 1852 was in use as a commercial photographer's studio, the extra light from the windows no doubt reducing exposure times and improving portraits. Next door, the **National Provincial Bank** (now NatWest) in Neo-Georgian styles dates from 1930 (George V – Windsor) Beyond, it becomes difficult to distinguish detail but nearly all date from the mid/late 1700s (Georgian), many with later alterations, mostly from the early 1800s (Regency). Some of the shop fronts are more modern.

No. 52

Castle Hotel

Nos. 15–17

No. 14

No. 13

National Provincial

19 *Nos. 47–50 High Street from Caleys*

This group, beyond the Guildhall, includes four buildings with some shared history. The fifth building, on the corner, though similar in style, is in Castle Hill and not included here (*See View 25*). Between Woods and the Guildhall is the Crooked House, just out of sight and described in *View 20*.

The four buildings all date from the 1500s or 1600s (Tudor/Stuart) and retain their original wooden frames which in the 1700s (Georgian) were refaced, new windows installed and (except No. 48) roofs or parapets added to modernise them, as was common practice at this time. **No. 47** is faced with brick (now painted) and topped by a slate covered mansard attic roof with dormer window. **No. 48** has retained its gable front while No. 49 and No. 50 have parapets to hide the original tiled roofs.

On **Nos. 48 & 49** the brickwork has been coated with stucco (smooth render). The shop front of **No. 49** is Victorian.

No. 50, Woods of Windsor, said to have been built in 1699 (Stuart), has a timber frame with stucco added about 1800 (Georgian/Regency). The windows have blind boxes, originally housing external blinds which could be pulled down to keep out the sun. The shop front dates from the 1800s. In 1770 the building was acquired by an apothecary (forerunner of a pharmacist) who supplied remedies to the townspeople and to Royalty, including George III. It remained a pharmacist's or chemist's shop from then on. In 1971 when Woods Pharmacy was sold, the new owners discovered ancient perfumery recipes, some dating back to the founding of the business. These were used to develop a new range of perfumery products, so successfully that they are now sold world-wide.

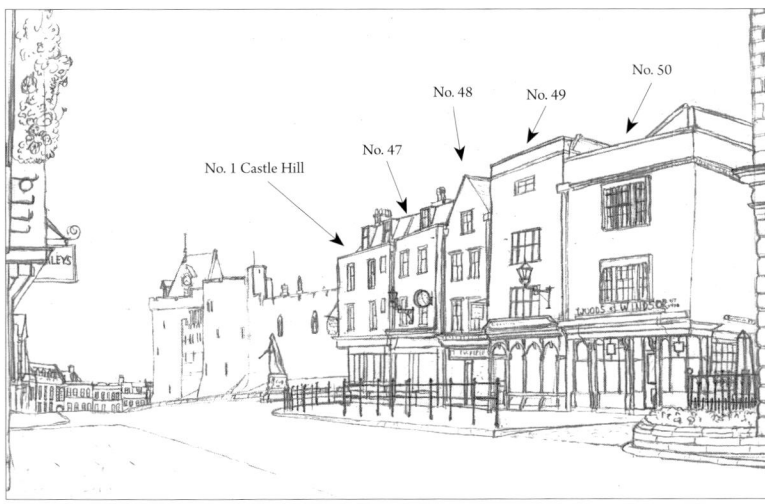

No. 50

No. 48

No. 49

No. 47

No. 1 Castle Hill

20 No. 51 High Street (Market Cross House/Crooked House) seen from Caleys

This small but interesting timber-framed building is popularly known as the **Crooked House** due to its very marked tilt. The current name, **Market Cross House**, sounds ancient though probably only dates from the 1900s. It started life as a butcher's shop, became a beer retailer's shop for a time, a public house 'The (Royal) Standard' and then passed through a succession of other occupiers before becoming a tea shop. Its history is the subject of debate as to building date and the reason why it has acquired its alarming

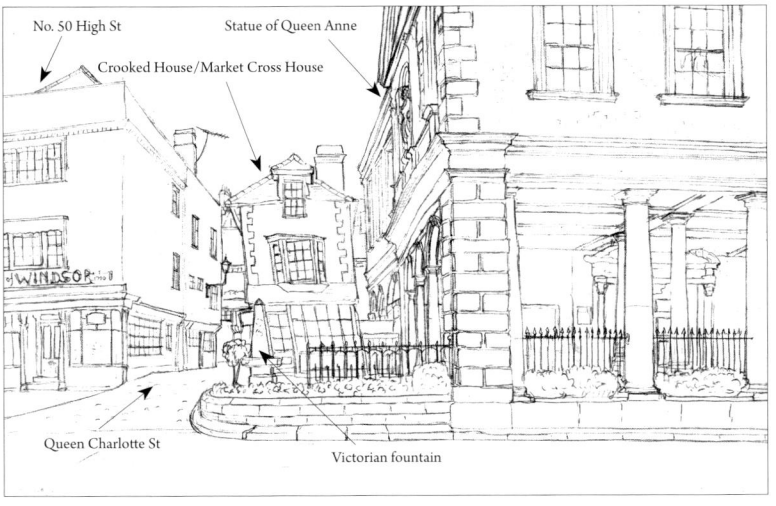

No. 50 High St — Crooked House/Market Cross House — Statue of Queen Anne — Queen Charlotte St — Victorian fountain

lean. The house stands very close to the Guildhall and the buildings have some shared history though details are muddled.

The house is in the ancient market area of Windsor and records show that an older building on this site was purchased by William Bradbury in 1656 (Stuart) – the area around was known as the butchers' shambles where several butchers plied their trade. The butcher's shop/dwelling passed through several generations of the same family and by 1718 it was owned by Silas Bradbury, William's great grandson. This older building was replaced by the existing one but there is some disagreement on the exact timing of events. Some say that the older building was demolished in 1686/7 when work began on construction of the new Market House (Guildhall) and the new one built sometime after 1690 *(Views 15 & 16)*. There appears to be more evidence that the older building stood until 1718 before being demolished in order to replace it. Just as the new building was about to be started, Windsor Corporation claimed ownership of the land but after a legal battle failed to prove it. Silas had the new house built sometime during 1718 but for the early Georgian period it was old fashioned, timber frames having been superseded by brick or stone many years earlier. Perhaps some of the old timber was re-used?

Why does the house lean? Theories abound. Perhaps unseasoned (green) oak was used which warped with age, though many dispute this. More likely the house is too tall and top heavy for a detached (and therefore unsupported) dwelling. It may have been supported by neighbouring buildings until 1828/29 when they were demolished to make way for the Guildhall extension and so only began leaning after that date. The Corporation had tried to purchase the dwelling (for demolition) at that time but the asking price was too high.

Will the house ever fall over? It is unlikely since it was apparently reinforced with steel during refurbishment around 1980. The diminutive size of the building and its proximity to the Guildhall is very apparent in this view. The statue of Queen Anne looks out from the niche at the northern end. There is a Victorian drinking fountain in front of the house.

21 *No. 51 High Street (Crooked House), Queen Charlotte Street and Market Street*

This view shows the rear of the **Crooked House/Market Cross House** *(View 20)* and the dramatic lean of the building. Next door is the rear of the **Guildhall Extension** *(View 16)* with rear access to the first floor (fire escape?). The proximity of the two buildings can be seen. On the right is **Queen Charlotte Street** leading towards the **High Street**, with one of the **Caleys** store buildings visible directly ahead *(View 22)*. Named after Charlotte, wife of George III (both of whom enjoyed living in Windsor), it is claimed to be the shortest street in England at 51 feet 10 inches (16 metres).

To the left is **Market Street** (once known variously as Butcher Row, The Shambles and Queen Street) one of the ancient market streets which runs from Castle Hill to Church Lane.

In the left foreground is the **Carpenters Arms** public house built in about 1515 (Tudor) but with a façade (frontage) from about 1900 (late Victorian/Edwardian). It has entrances on Market Street (seen here) and Church Street *(View 30)*.

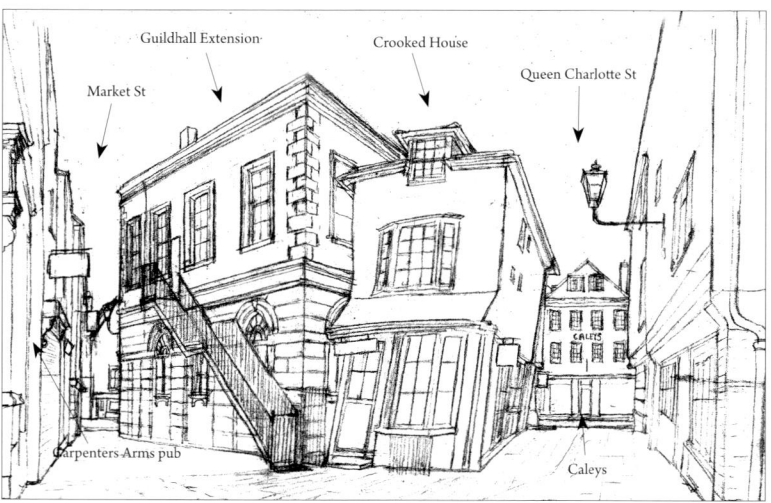

22 *Caleys Department Store, Nos. 19–23 High Street*

Caleys Department Store as seen a few weeks before closure in July 2006, with window displays of ladies' hats and outfits for Royal Ascot Week. In 1813 (Regency) Maria Caley, her brother John (a silk mercer) and her elder sister Charlotte, were running a millinery and dressmaking shop in Castle Street (now Castle Hill). Later, with John Caley and his wife Mary Ann now in charge, the business moved in 1823 to **No. 19 High Street**, next to the Castle Hotel and opposite the Guildhall. This is the pink painted building to the left of the picture, displaying the Royal Warrants. In 1919 it was bought by Selfridge

No. 19   No. 20   Nos. 21/22   No. 23

Provincial Stores, who in 1940 sold it to the John Lewis Partnership (another family-run business) with whom it continued as a department store until closure, still trading as Caleys. As the business grew it spread into three adjacent properties (Nos. 20, 21/22 & 23) resulting in a store with departments on several levels connected by small stairways. To some this was charming but to others (including the owners) it was inconvenient and helped lead to its demise. The store is still missed by former customers. Many Royal Warrants were gained, starting early on with Queen Charlotte (wife of George III) and at closure Warrants from HM Queen Elizabeth, the Queen Mother (wife of George VI) and HM Queen Elizabeth II were still proudly displayed on the frontage.

The main building **(No. 19)** originally late 1700s (Georgian/Regency) was refaced in 1951/2 as a near copy of the original – photographs from the 1920s show it looking remarkably similar to its current appearance except that the bay* on the far left was unevenly spaced with the other five. The alterations evened up the spacing and may have removed a doorway below the odd bay. The first floor French windows have balconettes (cast-iron 1800s – Regency). **No. 20** next door is from the late 1700s (Georgian/ Regency) also with French doors and a cast-iron Regency Gothick pattern balcony. The stuccoed (rendered) yellow building **(Nos. 21/22)** has a timber frame from the 1600s (Stuart), altered in early 1700s (Georgian). The upper floors overhang the modern shop front and the tiled roof has dormers. **No. 23** is from the early 1800s (Georgian/ Regency).

Since closure there have been great changes. The frontages were retained, with some ground floor alterations, but the buildings behind were demolished and replaced in 2010 by a large hotel (MacDonald Windsor) with T K Maxx department store and a coffee shop occupying the ground floors of Nos. 19–22 and the hotel entrance at No. 23.

*A bay is the term used to describe a vertical division of a building as indicated by a feature such as a window.

23 *High Street, looking south from corner of Peascod Street*

The north frontage of the **Guildhall** is seen here with the statue of Queen Anne in the niche, added in 1707. During restoration of the Guildhall in 1951 a main supporting beam was found, made from a single oak tree and part of the original 1690 structure. This strong beam or joist reinforces the council chamber floor above the open corn market and further explains why no extra pillars were required to support it *(View 15)*.

On the right can be seen the **Castle Hotel** *(View 13)*, some of the buildings of Caleys store *(View 22)* and in the foreground **No. 24** (now Cath Kidston) and part of **No. 25** (**HSBC Bank**) *(View 37)*.

No. 24 High Street was built about 1730 (early Georgian) but has a modern shop front. The upper windows have segmental arches (curved tops but not full arches) and the red brickwork is patterned with black vitreous bricks.

24 *Castle West End Wall in winter sun from No. 25 High Street (HSBC Bank)*

This view shows the West End Wall of the castle (Lower Ward) as seen on a sunny winter afternoon with shadows cast from the buildings opposite.

The statue of **Queen Victoria** stands on the site of the old Market Cross located at a focal point in the town, the junction of the four main streets. The cross was erected in 1380 (Richard II – Plantagenet) by John Sadler and removed in 1691 (William III – Stuart), just after the Guildhall was built. The site has long been used for proclamations including those for new Sovereigns (the most recent being HM Queen Elizabeth II in 1952). The history of the Statue is covered in *View 26*.

The three towers and curtain wall make up the **West End Wall**, built in 1227–30

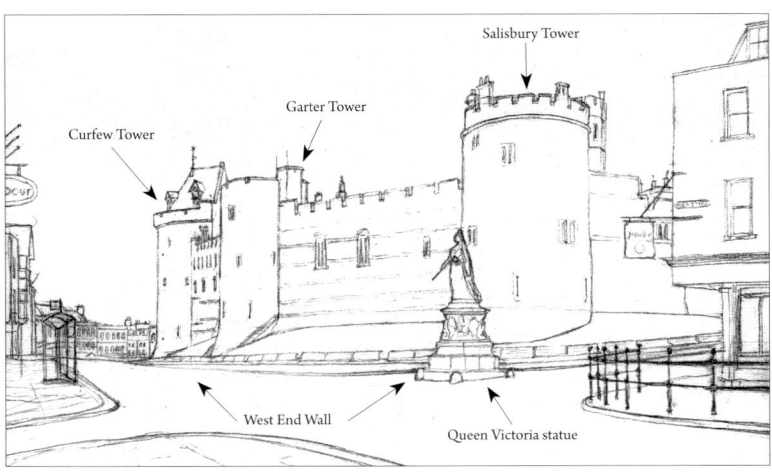

Salisbury Tower

Garter Tower

Curfew Tower

West End Wall

Queen Victoria statue

by Henry III (Plantagenet). This section of wall completed the stone fortification of the castle which had started out as a wooden structure when first created in 1070 by William I (The Conqueror). The art of castle building evolved over time and by this period it was evident that rounded towers (which had no 'weak-point' corners) were structurally more resistant to attack than square ones. These three are D-shaped and named, from left to right, the **Curfew** (with roof), **Garter** and **Salisbury** towers. This new section of stone wall extended the castle perimeter outwards and was built on the site of the old castle ditch. A new ditch was required, resulting in the demolition of houses and displacement of town's people who were compensated for their loss by the King. Further widening of the ditch took place soon after and by the late 1240s was about 80 feet (25 m) wide. Over time its defensive role declined and in the late 1600s (Stuart) was filled in and houses subsequently built on the site. By the 1800s buildings lined and obscured the castle wall from the Henry VIII Gate down to the bottom of the hill (Hundred Steps area). Some were destroyed by fires in the early 1800s but those remaining were removed in the early 1850s by Anthony Salvin, architect to Queen Victoria and Prince Albert, an action authorised by the Town Improvement Act 1848.

The towers have seen changes over the centuries but the curtain walls linking them still include much original work except for the windows and the top sections and battlements, the latter (lighter coloured and neater looking) added in the 1800s. Despite these alterations, this section of the castle retains more of its original 'fortress' character than the parts given major makeovers by Sir Jeffry Wyatville in the reigns of George IV and William IV (Regency).

25 *Castle Hill in morning sun from corner of Peascod Street/High Street*

Castle Hill is seen here in morning sun with, from left to right, the **Salisbury Tower** *(View 27)*, **Queen Victoria statue** *(View 26)*, **Henry VIII gate** *(View 33)* and in the background the **Round Tower** *(Views 5 & 31)*. These are described more fully in close-up views of each building as we proceed up Castle Hill. A capped turret of **St George's Chapel** (west end) *(Views 59 & 63)* is visible above the wall to the left of the picture.

Castle Hill is an ancient street. At one time known as Kings Market Place, it became Castle Street in the late 1700s (Georgian) and Castle Hill in about 1850 (Victorian). It was part of a route (footway) passing close to the castle towards London via Datchet,

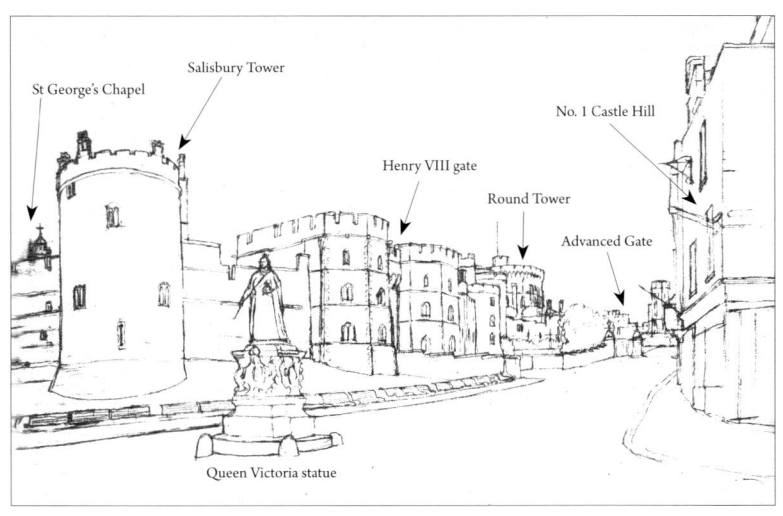

St George's Chapel
Salisbury Tower
No. 1 Castle Hill
Henry VIII gate
Round Tower
Advanced Gate
Queen Victoria statue

where there was a Thames river crossing *(Map 11)*. The ferry at Datchet was replaced by a toll-free bridge in 1707, paid for by Queen Anne. Windsor Corporation, which charged tolls on the bridge in Windsor, complained and was compensated for loss of revenue from government coffers. Datchet Bridge underwent many repairs and replacements over the years until, in the 1830s (Regency) a lack of co-operation between the counties of Berkshire (south side) and Buckinghamshire (north side) resulted in an ugly half iron and half wooden hybrid which was described as a 'hideous monstrosity'. The bridge was demolished in 1850 when the Windsor Improvement Act 1848 saw new roads and bridges linking Windsor and Datchet routed round rather than through the castle precincts (Home Park). The public route via Castle Street, which had already been restricted following the remodelling of the Upper Ward *(View 3)* and the building of the Advanced Gate *(View 31)* for George IV in the 1820s, now became redundant and the street was renamed Castle Hill.

The building on the right, **No. 1 Castle Hill**, forms the corner with the High Street and is part of the group described in *View 19*. Originally a timber framed building from 1500/1600s (Tudor/Stuart) it was altered in the 1700s (Georgian) by being faced with mathematical tiles* (now painted) and topped by a slate mansard attic roof with dormers. The ground floor is more modern, probably Victorian. It was run as a butcher's shop by John Bedborough from late 1800s/early 1900s (Victorian/Edwardian) and later became a restaurant, a china shop and is now an ice cream parlour/cafe.

*Mathematical tiles were used in Georgian times to reface (and so modernise) timber framed buildings as an alternative to brick refacing. The tiles are shaped to overlap each other with the exposed part shaped like a brick. When nailed in rows to a vertical wooden surface they give the appearance of a brick face. Their use is shown by the irregularities of the surface (where tiles have been pushed out of true) when compared to the brick refacing of No. 47 High Street next door *(View 19)*.

26 Queen Victoria Statue

The **statue of Queen Victoria**, erected to celebrate her Golden Jubilee (50 years since her accession to the throne on 20 June 1837) was unveiled on 22 June 1887 with the Queen in attendance. It cost £2,500, paid for by the people of Windsor and surrounding areas. Queen Victoria, who reigned until 1901 (over 63 years), was fond of Windsor and spent much of her time in residence here, in preference to London.

The statue was designed and created by one of Britain's leading sculptors, (Sir) Joseph Edgar Boehm, RA (knighted soon after the statue was unveiled). Born in Vienna to Hungarian parents in 1834, he was educated there before coming to Britain in 1862 to further his studies. He became a naturalised British citizen in 1865. The Queen

commissioned him to create bronzes of her family and statues at Windsor Castle. He died in 1890, three years after the statue was created.

The statue and the metal section of the pedestal are cast in bronze (an alloy of copper and tin). The statue was painted black in 2002 to mark the Golden Jubilee of HM Queen Elizabeth II but this has gradually worn to reveal a natural green patina, a thin tarnish of coloured copper salts on the bronze caused by reaction of the metal with chemicals in the atmosphere. The remaining parts of the pedestal are carved from Aberdeen red granite. The figure stands 15 feet (4.5 metres) high and shows the Queen in regal attire, holding the orb and sceptre and wearing the Ribbon of the Garter. She wears a small crown made for her in 1870 on her return to public life after a period of intense mourning for her husband, Prince Albert, who died in 1861. She found the large Imperial State Crown too heavy and difficult to wear with her mourning veil. It was first worn at the State Opening of Parliament in 1871.

The metal section of the base is decorated on each corner with images of fish and putti (winged small child figures similar to cherubs – *singular* – *putto*). Shield-like panels on each face of the plinth depict the Royal coat of arms on the front, Windsor's coat of arms on the back and, on the sides, panels '*To Commemorate the Fiftieth Year of the Glorious Reign of Victoria, Queen and Empress*' and a list of towns and villages whose residents contributed to the cost of the statue.

27 *Salisbury Tower and West End Wall from Castle Hill*

The **Salisbury Tower** (formerly Chancellor's Tower) stands at the southern corner of the West End Wall, the junction of High Street and Castle Hill. Like the Garter and Curfew towers, also seen here, it was built in 1227/30 by Henry III (Plantagenet) to a D-shaped plan, the curved face being better able to withstand mining and other siege techniques when compared to rectangular or square structures. This section of wall completed the stone fortification of the castle which had started out as a wooden structure when first created in 1070. When it came to replacing wood with stone, which began in earnest about 1170 (Henry II – Plantagenet), greater priority was initially given to the keep (Round Tower) the middle and upper wards (with Royal apartments) and the north wall of the Lower Ward.

The **Salisbury** and **Garter Towers** derive their names from their use as residences by Officers of the Order of the Garter. The Bishops of Salisbury traditionally held the role of Chancellor while the Garter Tower takes its name from The Garter King of Arms. The Most Noble Order of the Garter (the oldest and highest Order of Chivalry in the United Kingdom) was founded by Edward III in 1348. Membership was limited to 26 Knights Companion always including the Sovereign, the Prince of Wales and (up to) 24 others. The original knights were chosen for their exceptional military skills and loyalty to the king. Ladies were also associated with the Order but not as full members until quite recently. Some Officer roles (Prelate, Register and Usher) were established at the outset and others added by subsequent monarchs, that of Garter King of Arms by Henry V in 1415 and Chancellor by Edward IV in 1475. The names of these towers therefore date from after this time rather than when they were first built.

The Salisbury Tower was altered over time and is shown in a watercolour by Paul Sandby c. 1760 with large gothic-style windows on the upper storey and topped by a sloping tiled roof. The present appearance was largely created by Edward Blore in the 1840s (Victorian), an architect who followed on from Sir Jeffry Wyatville (1820s to 1840) but before Anthony Salvin began work on the castle around 1850. Blore removed the roof, raised the height of the tower another storey and added the turret and battlements to restore some of its original character.

Salisbury Tower

Garter Tower

28 *Castle Hill with Drums and Pipes of the Irish Guards*

Castle Hill is seen here on a cold and dull February day, the castle reflecting the mood as it usually does.

From this viewpoint can be seen a section of castle wall (between the Mary Tudor Tower and Henry VIII gate) quite different in character to the Heath stone used to face much of the castle. Creamy yellow oolitic limestone (originally from Caen in northern France) was used by Mary I (Tudor) in 1557 to build new **residences for the Poor Knights of the Order of the Garter** (*View 31*). The stone was taken from Reading Abbey (about 14 miles/22 km from Windsor) when it was being dismantled following

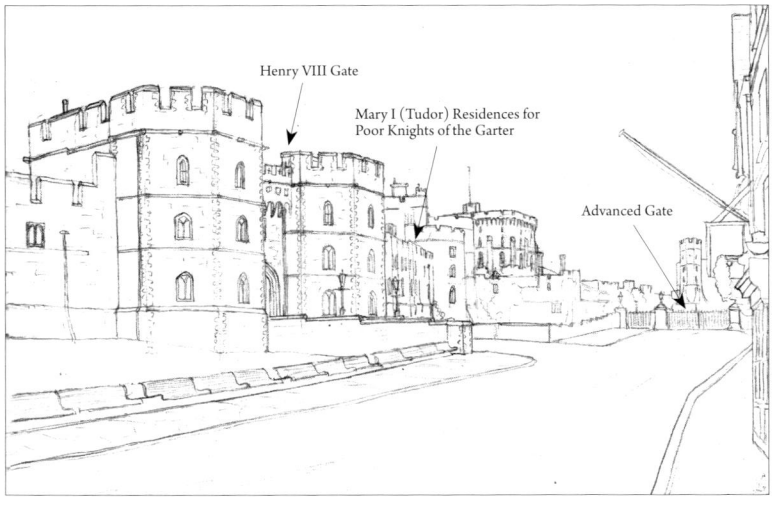

Henry VIII Gate

Mary I (Tudor) Residences for Poor Knights of the Garter

Advanced Gate

its dissolution and forcible closure in 1538 by Henry VIII, Mary's father. The Abbey was the burial place of Henry I (Norman) who had founded it in 1121.

The (Old) Guard dressed in grey winter greatcoats, leaves the castle through the **Henry VIII Gate** (*View 33*) towards the Victoria Barracks in Sheet Street. In the foreground we see the **Drums and Pipes of the Irish Guards** led by their **Irish wolfhound mascot**.

The Irish Guards were formed in 1900 by order of Queen Victoria in recognition of heroic actions by Irish troops in the Boer War (South Africa). They are affectionately known as 'The Micks'. The standard red-tunic ceremonial uniform is similar to the other Foot Guards, the Irish Guards wearing buttons in fours, a blue plume on the right side of the bearskin cap and a shamrock on the collar badge. The Regimental Band is similar in structure and appearance to those of other Guards regiments (*Views 12 & 13*) but the Irish (and Scots) Guards also have pipe bands. The Irish Guards ensemble is known as the 'Drums and Pipes' rather than the Scots Guards 'Pipes and Drums'.

The pipers wear saffron kilts, dark green tunics and cloaks and a cap called a caubeen with the badge pointed towards the piper's right eye. In the early years of the Regiment they played two-drone pipes (Great Irish Warpipes) but now play the Army standard three-drone Scots Highland pipe.

The mascot, looked after by a Drummer, leads the Regiment on all parades. There is only one mascot at any time, each given a name associated with a High King or Legendary Chieftain of Ireland. The mascot shown here is named Conmael after a son of Eber Finn, a King of Ireland. He made his debut at the Trooping of the Colour ceremony in 2009.

29 *Market Street and the Horse & Groom*

Moving up the south side of Castle Hill to its junction with Market Street we come to No. 4 Castle Hill, the **Horse & Groom**, an old timber-framed structure from the 1500s (Tudor) which has been a public house for nearly three hundred years. The first publican's licence is from 1719 (when it was called the Lower Rose & Crown) though it was probably a drinking establishment prior to this. In 1792 (Georgian) the name was changed to the Horse & Groom and in 1837 it was sold to brewers Neville Reid & Co, who were later bought out by Noakes & Co then Courage & Co *(View 51)*.

The building has a large gable with a tile hung upper portion, patterned barge boards, an old tiled roof and upper floors jettied over the ground floor (overhanging). Part of the

cellar extends beneath Castle Hill. This was once a passage/tunnel leading towards the castle but now filled in and ending in a blocked-off arch. Inside, the public house has an ambience in keeping with its ancient history.

The building to the left, **Nos. 10/11 Castle Hill**, will be described in *View 34*. On the right is **No. 3** *(View 35)*.

Between these buildings is **Market Street** (once known variously as Butcher Row, The Shambles and Queen Street) one of Windsor's ancient market area streets which leads to Church Lane. Along this street on the left is the sign for the Carpenters Arms public house *(Views 21 & 30)*. The rear of the **Guildhall Extension** can just be seen at the far end *(View 21)*.

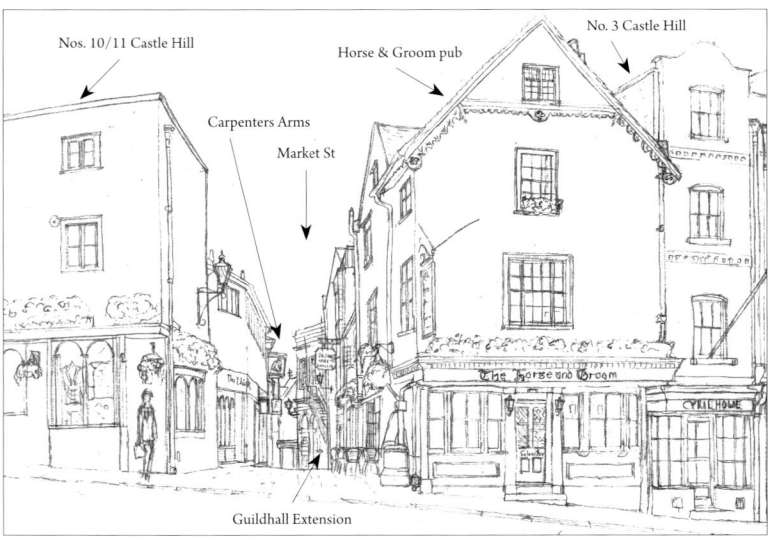

Nos. 10/11 Castle Hill

No. 3 Castle Hill

Horse & Groom pub

Carpenters Arms

Market St

Guildhall Extension

30 *Church Street from Castle Hill*

Church Street runs parallel to Market Street a little further up Castle Hill, opposite Henry VIII Gate, and leads to Church Lane. As part of the old market area where fish were sold it was known formerly as Fish Street. The name changed about 1780 (Georgian).

On the left we see the side of **Castle Hill House** (*View 34*) with steps leading down to the basement. Further along on this side are a number of interesting buildings from the 1500s and 1600s (Tudor/Stuart) some with later additions and altered fronts, particularly where shops have been inserted. Just visible near the lamp are the projecting bays of **Nos. 5/6**, now divided but once a single building dating from the 1600s (Stuart). **No. 5** is known as **Nell Gwyn's House** where it is claimed that Charles II's most famous mistress once lived, though many doubt this story. **No. 7** next door, a Tudor timber-framed inn called the **Kings Head**, has a copy of Charles I's death warrant on a large panel above the front door.

At the far end, on the corner with Church Lane, **Nos. 8/9** is a Tudor building with an added early 1700s (Georgian) frontage, once the Windsor Royal General Dispensary (*View 17*).

Facing the end of the street is a Georgian/Regency inn, formerly the **Ship Inn** (Hotel) and now called **The Blarney Stone** (*View 17*). The tower of the **Parish Church (St John the Baptist)** (*View 14*) is seen behind. Working across we come to **Nos. 12/13**, a large brick building (four storeys and basement) from the late 1700s (Georgian/ Regency) divided into two dwellings/shops with curved bay windows on the first floor of each. Next to this is the **Carpenters Arms** public house, which also has an entrance on Market Street. The building dates from 1515 (Tudor) with a frontage probably from about 1900 (late Victorian/Edwardian). The facade (at least) of the yellow painted building on the right is modern.

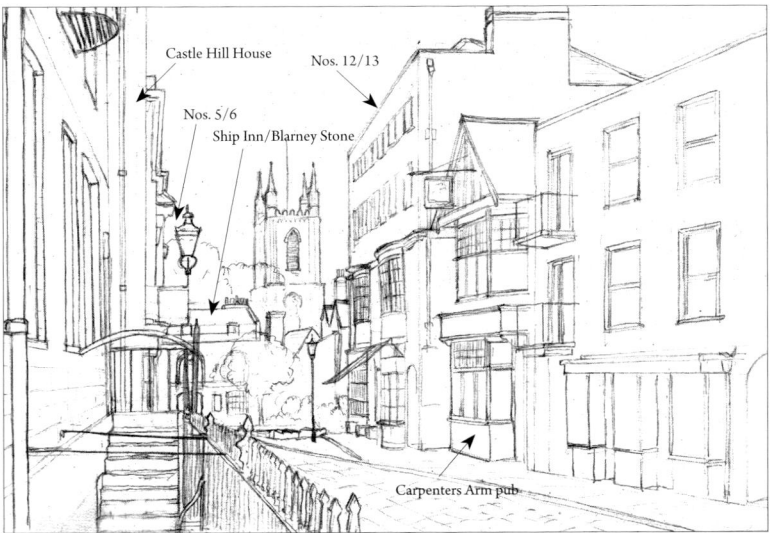

Castle Hill House

Nos. 12/13

Nos. 5/6

Ship Inn/Blarney Stone

Carpenters Arm pub

31 *Round Tower and Advanced Gate*

This view is from the corner of St Albans Street and Castle Hill. In the foreground is the **Advanced Gate**, added by Sir Jeffry Wyatville in the 1820s (Regency) for George IV. On the right (out of sight) is the modern ticket office and public entrance to the castle.

The **Round Tower** has seen many changes. The original keep (or donjon) was built about 1070 (William I – Norman) as a wooden palisade or tower on an artificial chalk mound (or motte). Its primary roles were a refuge in times of war, a lookout post and perhaps a prison. A century later in 1170 (Henry II – Plantagenet), with the mound now compacted enough to take its weight, came a circular shell-keep built in stone. Following a siege in 1216 (John – Plantagenet) part of the mound subsided and the keep was rebuilt about 1220 (Henry III – Plantagenet) not quite circular and with a flattened side. The most dramatic change came much later in 1828/32 (Regency) when Sir Jeffry

Wyatville raised its height by 30 feet (9 metres) and added the Flag Turret. Master mason James Bedborough (*Views 13 & 17*) used a Heath stone facing (*View 5*) with Bath stone dressings. This created the iconic shape by which the castle is best known today.

To the left of the Round Tower is the round-cornered **Henry III Tower** built about 1220 and altered around 1680 by Hugh May, architect to Charles II (Stuart). On the inner side (not visible here) are some his round arched windows, rare survivors as most of these (and other parts of his work) were later altered, first by James Wyatt (1800) and more extensively by his nephew Wyatville (see above) who also built the low building to its right, the **Saxon Tower**.

Further left, the high square **Mary Tudor Tower** (named as such in 1952) was built in 1360 (Edward III – Plantagenet) to house the bells of the first St George's Chapel. At the same time lodgings were created from here up to Henry III tower for the Priest Vicars (chapel choristers). In 1479 Edward IV (York) moved the bells to a new belfry in the Curfew Tower for his new St George's Chapel started in 1475 (*View 43*) and in 1481 the Priest Vicars moved to the Horseshoe Cloister (*View 48*). In 1557 under Mary I (Tudor) the tower became a residence for the Governor of the Poor (now called Military) Knights of the Order of the Garter while the Poor Knights themselves were housed both in the old Priest Vicars' lodgings and new residences built in the Lower Ward from here down to Henry VIII gate (the latter built from distinctive creamy yellow Caen stone taken from Reading Abbey following its dissolution by Henry VIII in 1538 – *View 28*). Mary, who had married King Philip II of Spain in 1554, had her own and her husband's coats of arms carved on the tower, one of the few places in England where King Philip's arms can be seen. The **(un-named) semi-circular tower** on the outer face of the wall is by Henry III (1220s).

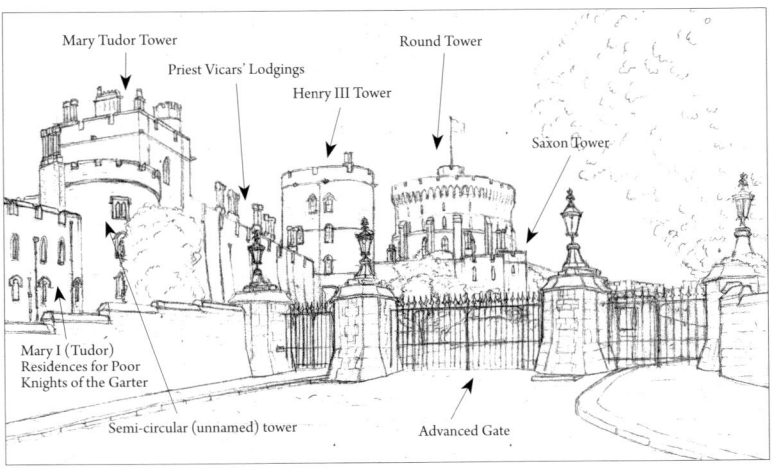

Mary Tudor Tower
Priest Vicars' Lodgings
Henry III Tower
Round Tower
Saxon Tower
Mary I (Tudor) Residences for Poor Knights of the Garter
Semi-circular (unnamed) tower
Advanced Gate

32 *Royal Free School (now Masonic Hall) and St Albans Street*

The old Royal Free School stands at the junction of Church Lane and **St Albans Street**, formerly Priest Street, which acquired its present name in the early 1800s (Regency). Charles II (Stuart) fathered many children though none with his wife (Catherine of Braganza) so left no legitimate (Royal) heirs. Charles Beauclerk his eldest son by his best known mistress, Nell (Eleanor) Gwyn, was made Earl of Burford and, in 1684, Duke of St Albans. He became a good soldier and, later, Lord-Lieutenant of Berkshire. Burford House was built for Nell Gwyn by the King, on land which later became the Royal Mews (see below). Charles Beauclerk and his heirs lived here until 1777 when the 3rd Duke sold it to George III after financial problems brought on by overspending.

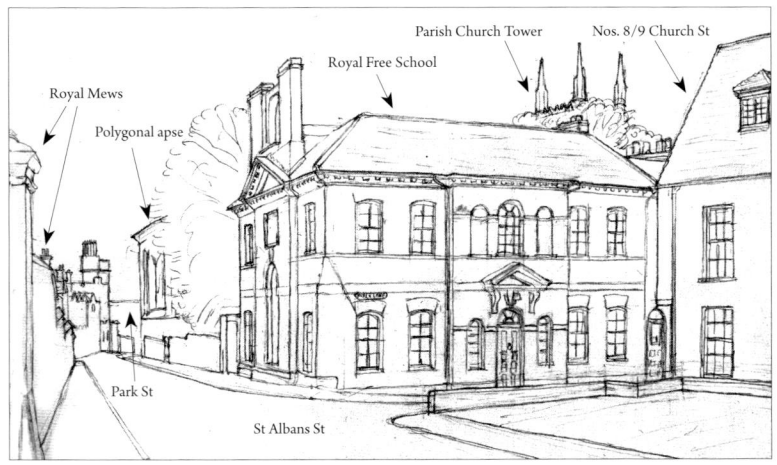

The idea for the **Royal Free School** to educate poor children took shape in 1705 with Queen Anne (Stuart) one of the principal benefactors. Classes were first held in the church but in 1724 Theodore Randue, one of the founders, left £500 in his will for the school seen here, built 1725/6 (Georgian). There is some (Baroque) influence of Sir Christopher Wren in its style but he could not have designed it, as some have asserted, because he died in 1723. The school, originally with 40 boy and 30 girl pupils, moved in 1862 (Victorian) to new premises and the building became the Masonic Hall. It is in dark red brick with a tiled roof, the eaves having a cornice with brick modillions (small closely spaced brackets). The central windows and niches have semi-circular heads. The front door has a semi-circular fanlight and a triangular hood (pediment and cornice) supported on brackets. A distinctive feature is the large chimney with two stacks joined by a 'flying' arch.

On the right is the rear of **Nos. 8/9 Church Lane**. This 1500s (Tudor) building (later altered) was at one time the Royal Windsor General Dispensary (*View 17*). Behind the school is the tower of **St John the Baptist Church** (*View 14*), and further down St Albans Street the **chancel and polygonal apse** added by Samuel Teulon in 1870 (*See View 4 for other buildings by this architect*).

Further down still on the left is a red brick building (1849 – Victorian) with large black doors, once a carriage shed for the **Royal Mews** and now a Learning Centre for children. The operational part of the Mews is behind the brick wall to the left of the picture and extends down most of the length of St Albans Street. The Mews (for horse stabling/training and storage for coaches /carriages) were designed by Sir Jeffry Wyatville for William IV in 1837 but not completed until 1842. **Park Street** (*View 10*) is just visible.

33 *Henry V111 Gate, Castle Hill and Harte & Garter Hotel*

From the top of **Castle Hill** we look down towards the **Henry VIII Gate** the main castle entrance (though the George IV Gateway in the Upper Ward built in the 1820s is now the Sovereign's entrance). Henry VIII (Tudor), famous for his six wives, liked Windsor and from the beginning of his reign in 1509 spent much time here. The gate, built around 1511 by mason Henry Smyth, replaced a gatehouse created by Henry III (Plantagenet) in 1240. The battlemented towers on each side have polygonal faces and above the entrance arch is a parapet with machicolations – open spaces between supporting brackets (corbels) through which objects or liquids could be dropped on

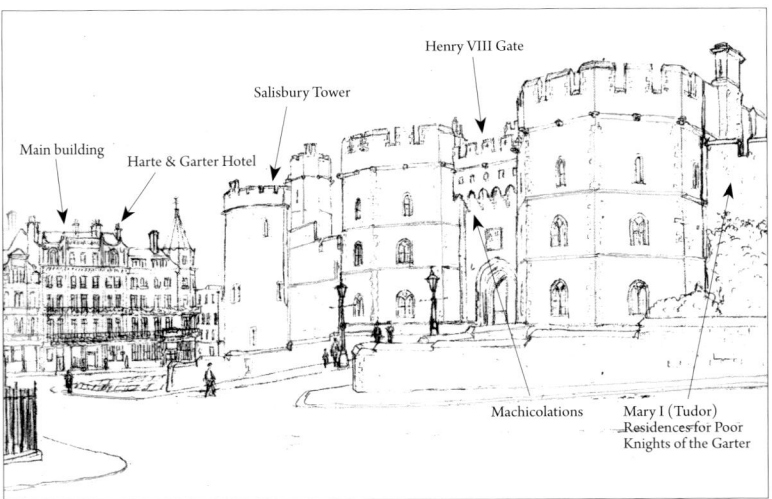

Henry VIII Gate

Salisbury Tower

Main building

Harte & Garter Hotel

Machicolations

Mary I (Tudor) Residences for Poor Knights of the Garter

to attackers. Above the arch is Henry's coat-of-arms and further up a row of carvings including Henry's Tudor rose and a pomegranate – symbol of Catherine of Aragon, his first wife. The windows are later additions, probably by James Wyatt (uncle of Sir Jeffry Wyatville) in the early 1800s (Georgian/Regency). Until the 1990s this was the main public entrance to the castle but now serves only as an exit. The **Salisbury Tower** with its turret is seen on the corner (*View 27*).

The red brick hotel in the High Street beyond is the **Harte & Garter Hotel**, formerly the White Hart Hotel. The two distinct sections of the building are well seen from here, making this a good time to discuss its building history. By the 1500s (Tudor) there were neighbouring taverns on this site, The White Hart and The Garter, both destroyed by fire in 1681 (Stuart) and rebuilt in 1682 as The White Hart. In the 1890s (Victorian) a major rebuild occurred, the details of which are made clearer by a study of contemporary photographs. In an 1889 photo the old four storey White Hart main building is seen and adjoining, to its right and at a slight angle, a three storey building (part of the same hotel). Both have first floor balconies. In 1890 the main building was replaced by the present one; one storey taller, the White Hart Hotel name panel at the top, large pilasters, and a second floor balcony. By 1895 the right hand building appears largely unchanged except that the ground floor now has the distinctive bracketed entrance seen today. Not long afterwards, in about 1897, the upper section was rebuilt, one storey taller and an octagonal turret (with terracotta decorations, pinnacle roof and weather vane) added to the corner.

A building adjoining to the right of this section of the hotel was demolished at this time. The Great Western Railway was rebuilding the Windsor Central station on a much grander scale for Queen Victoria's Diamond Jubilee in 1897, adding a large entrance arch (*View 40*) which required the approach road from the High Street to be widened, hence the removal of the building. The new hotel building was designed to complement the revamped station approach.

34 Castle Hill and Peascod Street from the Advanced Gate

We stand close to the Advanced Gate looking down **Castle Hill**. On the left, at the corner of **St Albans Street**, is **Castle Hill House**, a large town house from the late 1700s (Georgian/Regency). It was refaced in the mid 1800s (Victorian) with ashlar (smooth faced, tightly jointed stone) and various Victorian Gothic features added, such as the porch with stepped gables and pointed arch *(see also View 4)*. There is a slate covered mansard roof *(described View 9)*, the dormer gables being decorated with barge boards. The railings are Georgian. The building became The Vicarage for a while in the late 1800s/early 1900s (Victorian/Edwardian) and in the mid-1900s a nurses' home for the local King Edward VII hospital.

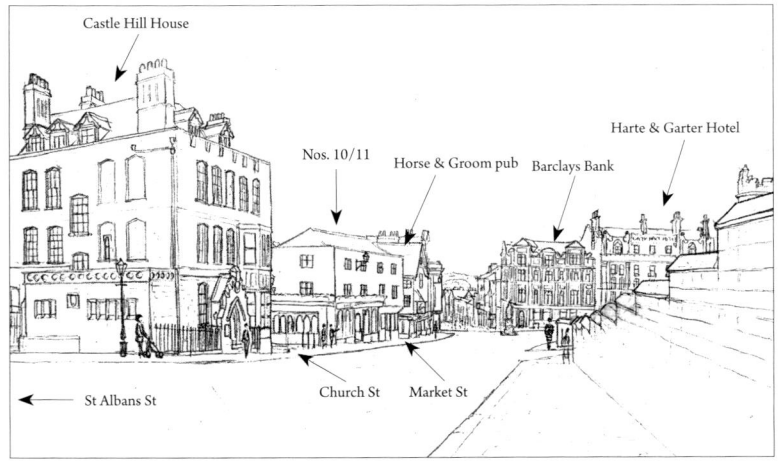

Church Street is to its right *(View 30)* then the blue painted **Nos. 10/11 Castle Hill** from the 1500/1600s (Tudor/Stuart) with a frontage from the early 1800s (Regency). This interesting shop front has arched windows and is decorated with Corinthian pilasters. Now occupied by the Edinburgh Woollen Mills, the building was a grocer's shop with Royal Warrants from the late 1800s (Victorian) until the mid-1900s. From about 1900 it was run by F Radford and by 1920 had become a Waitrose store (long before John Lewis Partnership bought the small shop chain in 1937) which it remained until about 1950. Next is **Market Street** and the **Horse and Groom** public house *(View 29)*.

Sloping down beyond the **Queen Victoria statue** *(View 26)* is Peascod Street, once part of an ancient thoroughfare which passed through Windsor from the west and continued up past the castle and onwards to Datchet ferry *(View 25)*. It derives its name from the growing of peas (an important food in mediaeval times) in a croft, the original name being something like Pescroft Strate (spellings were very variable in this period). It is now Windsor's main shopping street, pedestrianised in the 1990s. The twin-gabled building, just visible, is the old Edwardian front (1902) of **Daniels Department Store** which, since the demise of Caleys *(View 22)*, is now the only such store in Windsor. The old building was demolished and replaced by a new store with modern frontage in 2012.

On the corner, to the right of the statue is **Barclays Bank**, the building is from 1905 (Edwardian) in 'Northern renaissance' style with elements copied from Greek/Roman architecture. Next door is the **Harte & Garter Hotel** *(View 33)*.

35 *Castle Hill, High Street and Peascod Street from Henry V111 Gate*

Standing outside Henry VIII gate we look down Castle Hill to the High Street and Peascod Street.

In **Castle Hill**, the **Horse and Groom** public house **No. 4** is described in *View 29* and on the corner **No. 1** (with the wall lamp) in *View 25*. Between, we see **Nos. 2 and 3** both with frontages from the late 1800s (Victorian). **No. 2** is in deep red brick and topped by a (triangular) pediment and with a modern shop front. **No. 3** is a very narrow (one bay) building with a pinkish painted brick front and a gabled parapet. Charles

Knight and his son, also Charles, ran a printing and book shop at No. 2 Castle Hill (a former building) and in 1812 (Regency) published the first edition of the Windsor and Eton Express, a local newspaper which survives to this day. By 1898 the present building at No. 2 was occupied by Marshall – printer/bookseller/stationer and publisher of the Royal Windsor Guide.

In the High Street **Barclays Bank**, built in 1905 to replace two smaller buildings (*View 34*), stands next to the **Harte & Garter Hotel** (formerly White Hart) from 1890 (*Views 33 & 44*), the name panel and large pilasters (flat pillars) adorning the frontage being better seen in this view.

The building on the left-hand corner of Peascod Street **No. 27 High Street** is now occupied by Barbour, originally Burtons Tailors then Bally Shoes. It dates from 1935 in Neo-Georgian style with large (giant) pilasters on the Peascod Street side. Until 1933 there were two shops at this spot. Both were demolished and only the left hand one replaced with the present building, so allowing the top end of Peascod Street's busy thoroughfare to be widened.

89

36 *Salisbury Tower and Castle Hill from Barclays Bank*

Salisbury Tower (on the corner of the castle West End Wall) and Castle Hill are seen here on a rainy day.

Salisbury Tower (formerly Chancellor's Tower) was built in 1227/30 by Henry III (Plantagenet) as part of a major building programme in the Lower Ward *(View 27)*. It was restructured in the 1840s (Victorian) by Edward Blore who succeeded Sir Jeffry Wyatville as castle architect. Until the 1800s this view of the tower would have been obscured by buildings occupying the old castle ditch area – shops, inns or houses. A few on this corner were cleared away in the 1820s by Wyatville (for George IV), some

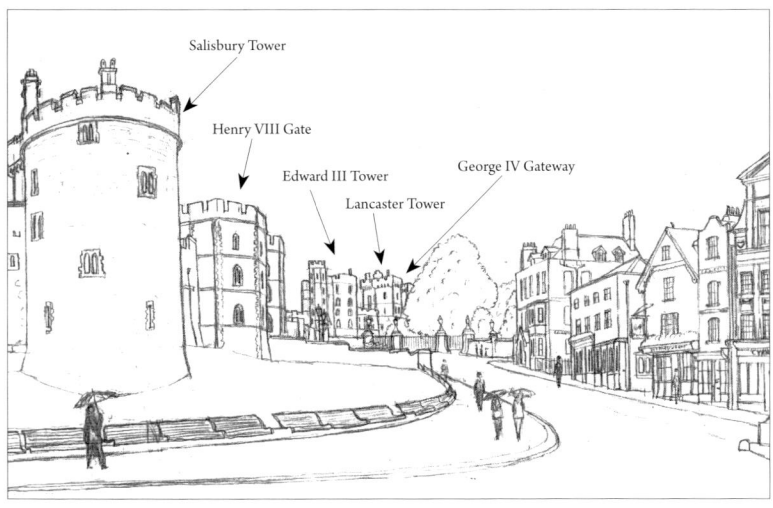

accidentally destroyed by fire and the remainder removed in the early 1850s as a result of the Windsor Improvement Act 1848, in part instigated by Albert, Prince Consort (husband of Queen Victoria). Largely funded by the railway companies who wanted to bring their lines into the town, this Act authorised changes to improve/alter the environs of the castle and town and to remove substandard housing and insanitary conditions. These houses would have discharged their waste close to the castle walls, not too pleasant for those occupying rooms above on this side of the Lower Ward. Following this clean up, the area occupied by the buildings was grassed over and a boundary wall built around its edge. The section of wall from Henry VIII Gate to the Curfew Tower was removed and replaced by seats in 1961 as part of a Civic Trust Project to improve the town's amenities and appearance.

From this angle it is possible to see buildings of the Upper Ward of the castle, namely Edward III Tower and Lancaster Tower (part of the George IV gateway). The **Edward III Tower**, originally known as the Devil's Tower because it was said to be haunted, was actually built by Henry III and is more or less contemporary with the Salisbury Tower. Like other towers built at this time it is curved in shape. A tall octagonal turret was added to its side in the 1820/30 period (Regency) by Sir Jeffry Wyatville. At this time Wyatville also created the **George IV Gateway** by building the new **Lancaster Tower** as a companion for the much older **York Tower** with an arched entrance between them *(View 3)*.

37 *Queen Victoria Statue and High Street from near Salisbury Tower*

This view looks across to the **statue of Queen Victoria**, erected in 1887 for her Golden Jubilee. The history of the statue is covered in *View 26*. The Queen is dressed in coronation robes and pointing her sceptre (part of the coronation regalia).

On the left is **No. 1 Castle Hill** *(View 25)*. Beyond is the **Guildhall** *(Views 15 & 16)* and in the High Street the **Castle Hotel** *(View 13)* and the four **Caleys** buildings *(View 22)*. Next on the right is **No. 24 High Street** with the blue shop front *(View 23)*.

Nos. 25/26 High Street, the taller building to the right of this, has not yet been described. It probably dates from the 1800s (Regency/Victorian) but the frontage has

undergone some alteration over the years. Rodgers and Denyer, milliners/dressmakers/drapers with Royal Warrants, occupied both No. 25 and No. 26 from the mid/late 1800s until the early 1900s when Denyer and Dyson carried on the business. Later, in 1915, Caleys briefly occupied No.25. Rodgers and Denyer famously employed the author H G Wells as a draper's apprentice in 1880. The reluctant 13 year old Herbert was sent there by his parents, who were struggling financially and could no longer afford to send him to school. He proved to be less than diligent, preferring to read books under his desk, and after a month was asked to leave. Soon afterwards he was sent to a Drapery Emporium in Southsea (near Portsmouth, Hampshire) and spent three unhappy years as an apprentice there. He later went on to write many books including *Kipps* (which drew upon his apprentice experiences and inspired the 1960s musical '*Half a Sixpence*') and science fiction classics *The War of the Worlds*, *The Invisible Man* and *The Time Machine*. The ground floor of **No. 25**, once a traditional shop front, was radically altered in 1919 when the Midland Bank (now HSBC) created the frontage with marble Doric columns seen today.

The Peascod Street side of the corner building **No. 27** (Barbour) is seen, with large (giant) pilasters adorning the 1935 Georgian-style building *(View 35)*.

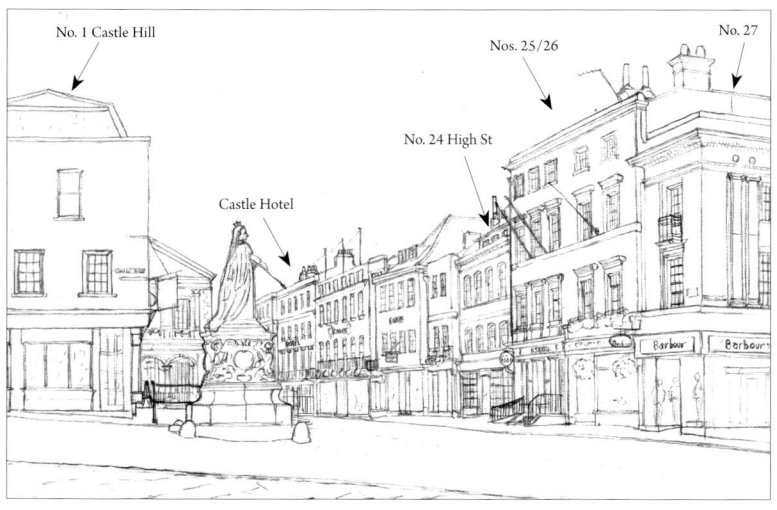

No. 1 Castle Hill · Nos. 25/26 · No. 27 · No. 24 High St · Castle Hotel

38 *Queen Victoria Statue with Life Guards Band*

This view is similar to *View 37* but includes the band of the Life Guards leading the (New) Guard along the High Street before they turn up into Castle Hill and through the Henry VIII gate.

The **Life Guards**, once a separate Regiment, was merged in 1992 with another Regiment, The Blues & Royals, to form the Household Cavalry Regiment (one of the six Regiments of the Household Division) though both retain their distinctive uniforms. They are stationed at Combermere Barracks on the outskirts of Windsor. The Life Guards wear red tunics and white plumes on their metal helmets while the Blues & Royals wear blue tunics and red helmet plumes. The full ceremonial uniform of the mounted soldiers includes a steel cuirass, comprising curved metal plates enclosing the upper body. It is the only remaining example of traditional metal body armour still worn by British soldiers. Mounted troops of the Regiment (stationed in London) can be seen in Windsor on State Visits when Heads of State from overseas are welcomed by HM Queen Elizabeth II and other members of the Royal family, usually one visit per year. The Band members are seen here in their red winter cloaks. Foot Guards, just visible behind, wear grey greatcoats during the colder months.

The Guard Change ceremony, when the New Guard marches through the town to the castle, takes place about 11 a.m. on alternate days for much of the year but in the mid-summer period is performed daily (though never on Sundays). The return trip to the barracks with the Old Guard is about half an hour later.

The buildings **Nos. 19–23 High Street**, once occupied by Caleys (*View 22*), are seen as they now appear (in 2014). The frontages were retained but the buildings behind were demolished and replaced by a large hotel, the **Windsor MacDonald Hotel**.

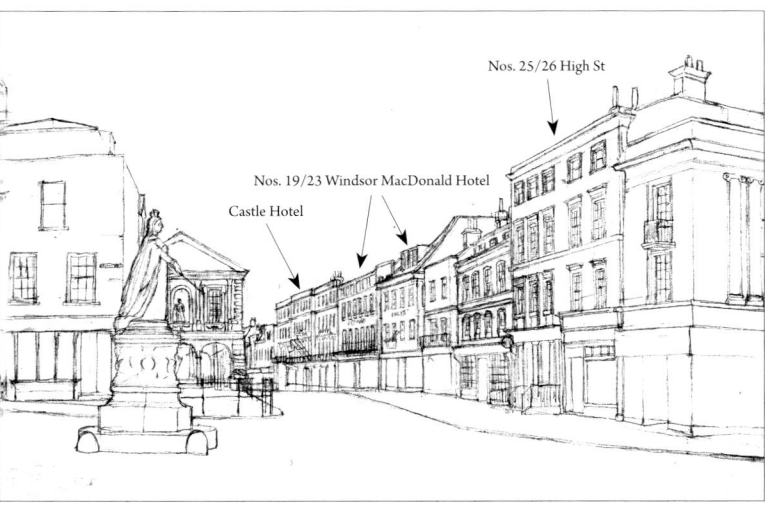

Nos. 25/26 High St

Nos. 19/23 Windsor MacDonald Hotel

Castle Hotel

39 *Garter Tower and Thames Street*

Standing outside the Harte and Garter Hotel we are at the point where High Street becomes Thames Street with the short road called Jubilee Arch (just out of sight on the left) forming the divide between the two. Until the early 1800s the meeting point of High Street and Thames Street was the (more logical) cross roads where the Queen Victoria statue now stands. **No. 1 Thames Street** with the red fascia (off-licence/liquor store) is seen on the left. Descriptions of the buildings in Thames Street will be found in later views.

The **West End Wall** of the castle is on the right with the **Garter Tower** in the foreground. This is the central tower of the three built by Henry III (Plantagenet) in 1227/30 to complete the stone fortification of the Lower Ward of the castle. Like the others it is D-shaped. The tower acquired its present name from association with the Most Noble Order of the Garter (founded by Edward III in 1348) and its use by the Garter King of Arms as lodgings during the three day annual Garter Festival *(View 27)*. The main ceremony was held originally on 23rd of April (the day commemorating St George – patron saint of England) but since 1948 Garter Day has been a one day event in June (on the Monday preceding the Royal Ascot racing festival).

The filling-in of the castle ditch in the later 1600s (after the 1660 Restoration of the Monarchy, in the reign of Charles II) gave greater opportunity for buildings to be put up along the entire length of this wall, so obscuring the lower parts of the castle and its towers. (Houses were here prior to this around the edge of the ditch, but not in such numbers). All these buildings were cleared away in the early 1850s as a result of the Windsor Improvement Act 1848, a scheme in part initiated by Prince Albert (Consort to Queen Victoria). By this time the once more revealed Garter Tower had fallen into-ruin, reduced to a shell, and was repaired and refaced about 1860 by architect Anthony Salvin.

The walls between the towers retain much of the original Henry III stonework (except the top sections) and include decorative banding with paler stone. The windows are of later date.

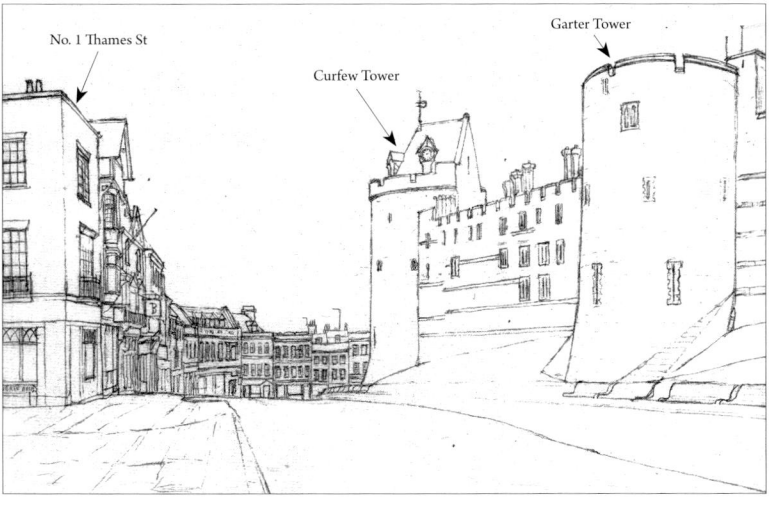

No. 1 Thames St

Curfew Tower

Garter Tower

40 *Jubilee Arch, Windsor & Eton Central Railway Station*

The short street now called **Jubilee Arch** was originally known as Station Approach when first built by the Great Western Railway. The archway was created as a grand approach to a new railway station built in honour of Queen Victoria's Diamond Jubilee in 1897. It replaced an earlier station on the same site designed and built by the renowned engineer Isambard Kingdom Brunel in 1849. The Great Western Railway (GWR) had raced to build a station ahead of its rival the London & South Western Railway whose terminus was (and still is) down the hill near the river. The companies originally faced

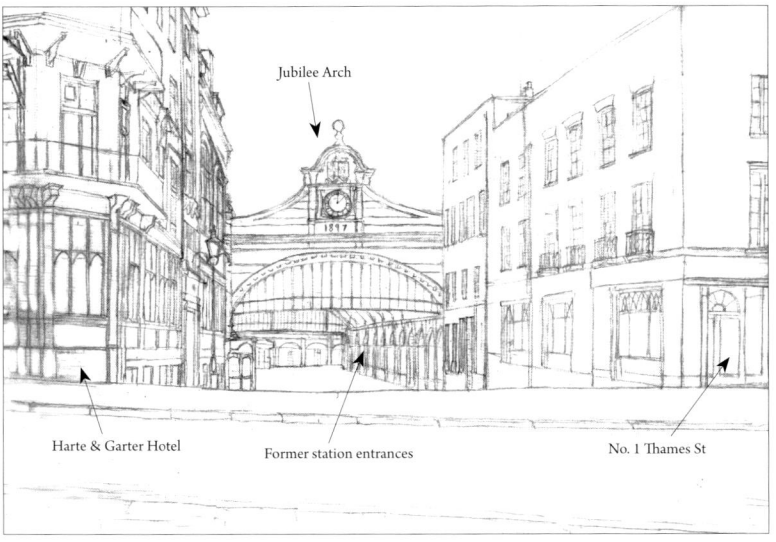

Jubilee Arch

Harte & Garter Hotel

Former station entrances

No. 1 Thames St

opposition from the Crown and Eton College but attitudes to rail travel, significantly by Prince Albert and Queen Victoria, gradually changed. After much debate and various financial deals which led to the Windsor Improvement Act 1848 both stations opened in 1849 with the GWR just ahead. A particular advantage to Royalty and the town was the clearance by the GWR of a vice-ridden slum in George Street which occupied the area through and beyond the archway. The station is the terminus of a short branch from the main line at Slough. The GWR from the outset used a broader gauge (track width) than all the other major British railway companies which, though with some advantages, proved so difficult to integrate into a nationwide system that they eventually switched to the standard gauge. The Windsor Branch started out as broad gauge, became mixed gauge in 1862 and standard gauge by the time the new station was built, so allowing a greater number of (narrower) lines to be laid than would otherwise have been the case.

Built on a grand scale fit for Royalty it originally had four platforms. The large glazed cab yard beyond the arch was added to protect passengers arriving and leaving by horse-drawn cabs. On the right are the former station entrances and booking hall. Above the arch clock is the GWR coat-of-arms incorporating shields of the cities of Bristol and London. The early railway company was spearheaded by Bristol merchants who wanted a direct and fast link to London. The arch, topped by a curved Dutch gable, once displayed the company's name in large letters where now we see Windsor Royal Shopping.

The adjacent section of the **Harte & Garter Hotel** on the left, then known as the White Hart Hotel, was also built in 1896/7 when the new station arch was created. At the same time a large building to its right was demolished in order to widen the approach to the new station. The building with the red fascia, **No. 1 Thames Street**, replaced Layton's Restaurant, a fashionable establishment demolished in the late 1930s. The rear, slightly taller, section with the flag is older. More of the station history is covered in *Views 41 & 42.*

41 *Windsor & Eton Central Railway Station (now also Windsor Royal Shopping)*

This view looks back towards the main building of the 1897 station created to commemorate Queen Victoria's Diamond Jubilee (60 years). It was originally called Windsor Station but later became **Windsor & Eton Central**. The **glazed canopy** over the cab yard seen in *View 40* is in the background. This is similar in design to the train shed canopies at London Paddington, the Great Western Railway's terminus, though at Windsor used to the side of rather than within the station. The main red brick building has an angled face and the station entrances and booking hall (now housing the Windsor

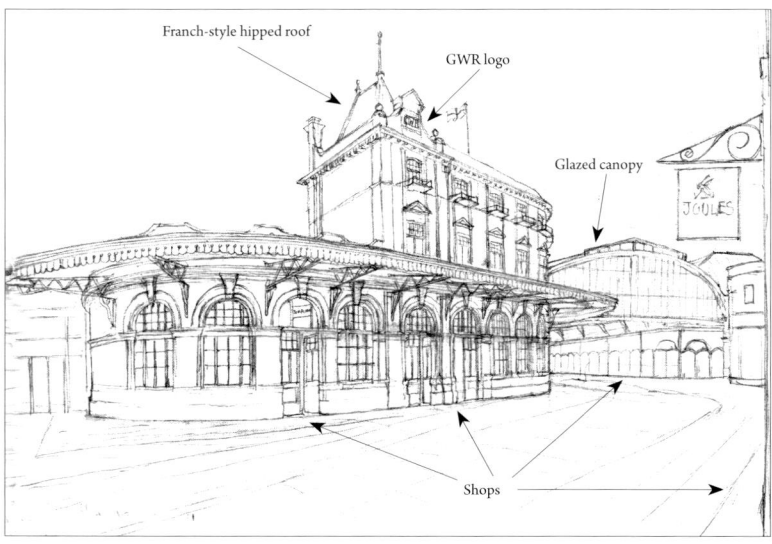

Information Centre) are out of sight around the corner beneath the canopy. It has a **French style hipped roof** and the **logo GWR** can be seen towards the top. This grand terminus originally had four platforms but in 1968/9, at a time when rail services in Britain were being slimmed down, three were taken out of service to leave just one, now shortened, platform. A well-used shuttle service still operates to and from Slough with good connections to other destinations including London, Oxford and Bristol.

There were also goods (freight) facilities at the station. Some were on the same level as the station platforms, beyond and left of the Royal waiting room (see below) and now used as a car park. A larger, low level yard (now a coach/car park) was accessed by a rail incline just outside the station *(View 42)*.

In 1979 part of the station was purchased by Madame Tussaud's and opened in 1982 as the Royalty and Empire exhibition. Using life size wax figures (some with sound and movement) this recreated aspects of Queen Victoria's Jubilee and her use of the station, including the arrival of the Royal train. The exhibition was based around the Royal waiting room, built in 1897 for the Sovereign's use and covered by another large glazed canopy (to allow ceremonial events to be protected from adverse weather). Both the building (now a restaurant) and the canopy survive, located to the left of the view seen here. The exhibition closed in the 1990s leaving 'The Queen', a replica GWR locomotive which proved too expensive to move, as a legacy. In 1997 the station was developed into a shopping and restaurant complex, putting this important building to new use while saving its structure. Some shops and eateries occupy original station buildings and others, such as those on the right, are housed in purpose built units.

42 *Bridgewater Terrace and Windsor & Eton Central Station*

This view from the junction of Bridgewater Terrace and Goswell Road shows the northern side of **Windsor and Eton Central station** (*Views 40 & 41*). In the distance can be seen the pointed turret of the **Hart & Garter Hotel** and the **Salisbury Tower**.

It demonstrates well that the centre of town is on a hill and that for easy passenger access from the High Street the station was raised on a wide brick viaduct. This was also necessary to keep the track above the river flood plain around the edge of Eton and at a high enough level for the bridge over the Thames as it approached Windsor. Eton College, initially opposed to the railway, also demanded a viaduct rather than an embankment on its land so

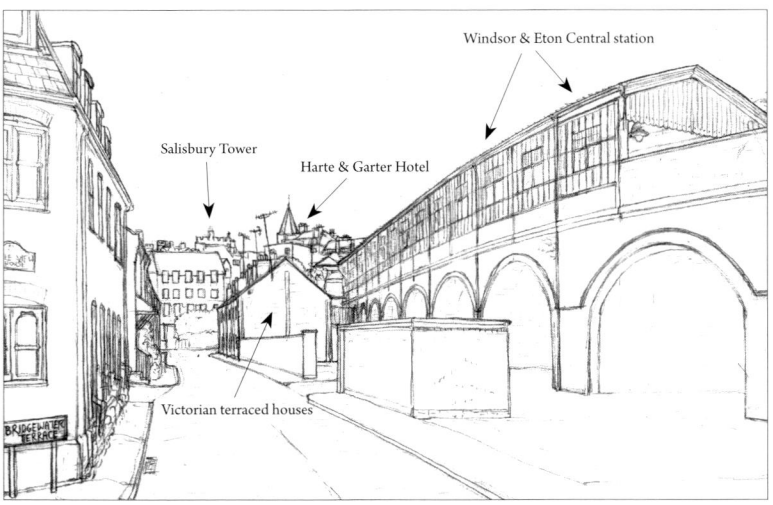

that boys could pass beneath it to access the river and their bathing places. When the line first came to Windsor in 1849 the viaduct was a timber construction but was replaced by brick from 1861–65. Though not spectacularly high, at over a mile (nearly 2 km) in length it is said to be among the longest rail viaducts in Britain, stretching from Windsor around the edge of Eton to beyond the Eton Wick road. Another Eton College stipulation was that the Thames river crossing had to be a single span, resulting in the distinctively shaped 'bow-string' bridge constructed of wrought iron by Isambard Kingdom Brunel (the Great Western Railway's engineer). Requiring some ingenuity to design and build it remains the world's oldest wrought iron rail bridge still in service.

Outside the station (and just behind this view) on the site of the present coach/car park was a goods (freight) yard reached from the viaduct by a steep backwards facing rail incline. Goods trains had to be taken more or less into the station, reversed down the slope and then taken forward into the yard. The upper part of this slope can still be seen near the coach park entrance. The town gas works on the other side of the viaduct was supplied with coal by a siding leading from the yard through one of the arches. Many of the larger arches are now occupied as business premises or by restaurants/clubs.

Bridgewater Terrace is Victorian, the terraced houses with tiny back yards at the far end dating from the late 1800s. Such housing is now rare in Windsor. The modern housing on the corner (with the road sign) replaced some cottages (in Tolladay Place) which were damaged beyond repair in late 1940 (WWII in the bombing campaign called the Blitz) when a bomb fell on a coal train in the nearby goods yard, propelling a coal truck into the roofs of the houses.

43 Thames Street and Curfew Tower

This view looks from the top of **Thames Street** which descends down towards the river, turning sharply right at the Curfew Tower and then left at the bottom of the hill near the Hundred Steps.

On the immediate left is **No. 2 Lloyds Bank**, an asymmetrical building from about 1890 (late Victorian) with two distinct halves in mock Jacobean style (imitation of early 1600s architecture) with timber framed frontage. The left side has a two storey oriel (higher-floor bay) window, the right a window with tent hood and wooden balustrade. The ground floor arched doors are flanked by wooden pilasters (flat pillars). Next door is the double gabled building **Nos. 3/4, the Duchess of Cambridge**, a public house, probably 1600s (Stuart) altered in the 1800s (Regency/Victorian). The stuccoed

(rendered) face has windows with (triangular) pediments while the ornate ground floor is fronted by pillars (in gold effect) and decorated with plaster bunches of grapes. The iron balconette is in the form of a grape vine. It was called The Grapes for over a century but, after many recent name changes, became the Duchess of Cambridge from 2011 in honour of Catherine (Kate) Middleton who received the title on her marriage to HRH Prince William, Duke of Cambridge on 29 April 2011. **W H Smith, Nos. 5/6**, is early 1700s (Stuart/Georgian) possibly timber framed with a slight jetty (overhang) but later re-fronted and stuccoed. It has a tiled roof with dormer windows and a prominent box cornice. **No. 18** further down the street (and not seen in other views) dates from 1730/40 (Georgian) with a Victorian shop front.

The **Curfew Tower** is one of the three built by Henry III in 1227-30 to complete the stone fortification of the Lower Ward. Of these it is the most prominent, due to its size and distinctive roof. Originally called the Clewer Tower (from the parish where the castle was established) it became the Bell Tower after installation of a massive oak belfry (bell-frame) and a bell chamber. This structure was created in 1479 (Edward IV – York) to house the bells of the new St George's Chapel (begun 1475) when they were moved here from the (now called) Mary Tudor tower *(View 31)*. The bell chamber (lead covered and topped by a dome) was prominent on top of the tower until 1863 (Victorian) when it was encased within the present roof by architect Anthony Salvin, part of a restoration/repair programme along the West End Wall in the mid-1800s. The new roof design (not universally approved of at the time) was inspired by the very similar one on the Tour de Tresau at Carcassonne in France, said to have been suggested by Emperor Napoleon III who visited Queen Victoria and Prince Albert in 1855 when the French walled city was being restored. For more history of the Curfew Tower see *Views 46, 48 & 50*.

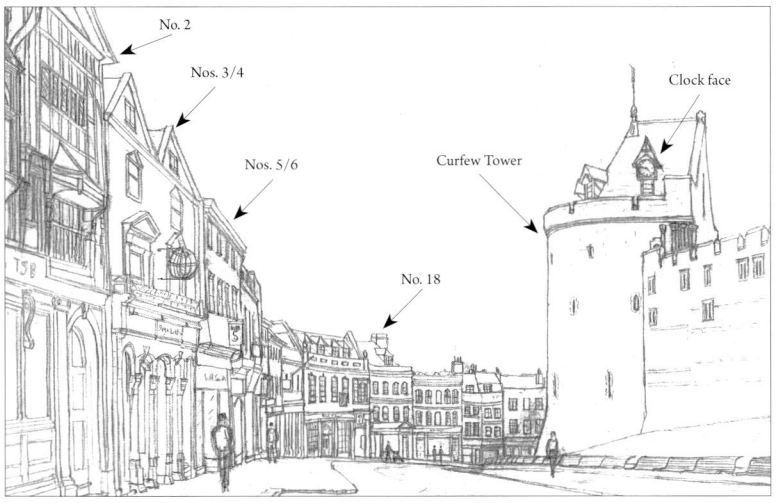

44 *Harte & Garter Hotel from Thames Street*

This view looks back up **Thames Street** from the castle side near the Garter Tower. Seats have replaced a stone wall which once bordered the grassed mound along the castle West End Wall. Originally erected in the mid-1800s after buildings along the old castle ditch were demolished as a result of the Town Improvement Act 1848, the wall was removed as part of another plan to improve the town's appearance and amenities, the 1961 Civic Project. On the left is the **Salisbury Tower** *(Views 27 & 36)*

Prominent is the **Harte & Garter Hotel** described in *View 33*. The hotel derives its name from two taverns in this location – The White Hart (the emblem of Richard

II – 1377–99) and The Garter (after the Order of the Garter/Garter Tower) both of which burned down in 1681 (Stuart) to be replaced by a larger White Hart. William Shakespeare's play, *The Merry Wives of Windsor* (written c. 1600) includes references to, and a scene set in, the Garter Inn. Some accounts say that he stayed in the inn while writing the play. It is also said that the play was written at the request of Queen Elizabeth I and that the first performance (for the Queen) took place inside the castle.

The rebuilding of the hotel is described in *View 33*. The main part of the White Hart was rebuilt in 1890 to replace the old hotel and by 1895 the frontage of the ground floor of the right hand section appears to have been replaced by the present one, though the floors above were unchanged. By 1897 the upper part of this section had been rebuilt, one storey taller and a large octagonal turret with terracotta decorations and distinctive pinnacle roof added to the corner. Balconies on the first and second floors are now joined across the entire frontage. When the new White Hart opened it was the first building in Windsor to have electric lighting. Here ends the **High Street**.

Jubilee Arch (formerly Station Approach) described in *View 40* forms the divide between here and **No. 1 Thames Street** (with red fascia). A building which stood to the right of the pinnacle turret was demolished to widen Station Approach when the new station was built around 1897.

The detail of **No. 2 Thames Street (Lloyds Bank)**, an 1890 (late Victorian) twin gabled building in Jacobean style is well seen here. The double oriel window to the left and the hooded window on the right are visible, along with the half-timber effect – see also *View 43*. It is possibly Arts and Crafts influenced *(View 6)*.

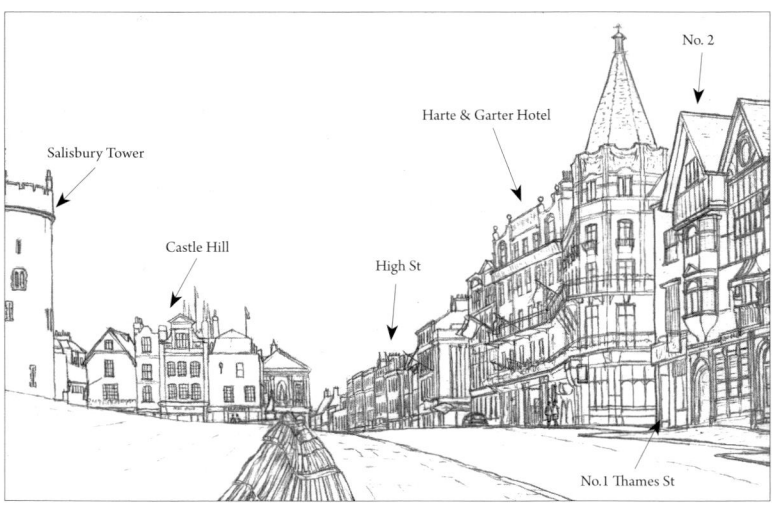

45 Thames Street from near the Curfew Tower

Looking back towards the **Harte & Garter Hotel** we have moved further down Thames Street to the point near the Curfew Tower where it curves round to follow the outline of the castle. From here the buildings in the upper part of the street can be better seen. The **Curfew** and **Garter Towers** are on the left. Though only one car is shown here, the left side of the street (where the seats are) is normally lined with taxis. In former times horse drawn cabs also plied their trade from here and metal wheel stops, to prevent carriage runaways down the hill, are still present along the kerb.

Starting at the top of Thames Street, four buildings **Nos. 1, 2, 3/4 and 5/6** have been described in *Views 40, 43 & 44*. The roof and dormers of **Nos. 5/6 (W H Smith)** can better be seen from this angle.

Next down **Nos. 7/8 and 9** are from early/mid 1700s (Stuart/Georgian). **No. 9** was occupied for many years by Royal Warrant holders Dysons the Jewellers who set a clock into the pavement outside the shop under a toughened glass window (apparently one of only three in the world). It was removed in the 1980s after the shop closed but a new one was installed in 2011. **No. 10** (Nandos) is early 1800s (Regency) with a tiled roof, flat-roofed dormers and a modern Regency-style shop front. This was also occupied by Dyson's but as a piano showroom. Next down, **No. 11** with the hipped tiled roof, is older, originally late 1600s/early 1700s (Stuart) but altered and stuccoed (rendered) in the mid 1800s (Regency/Victorian).

Nos. 12/12a dates at least to the early 1600s (Tudor/Stuart) but is probably older. It has a timber frame and the upper part was stuccoed in the 1800s (Regency). It was restored in 1971 particularly to the rear and there is a passage through between 12 and 12a to Curfew Yard behind.

46 Thames Street from the King & Castle (Wetherspoons)

From the first floor window of the King and Castle (now Wetherspoons – formerly Boots the Chemist) we look past Windsor Theatre towards the Hundred Steps Lodge where the street turns sharply left. It shows how Thames Street follows the line of the castle before heading for Windsor Bridge.

On the right is the lower part of the **Curfew Tower** (*Views 43, 48, 50*) showing the battered plinth at the base (battering is a widening and thickening of the lower wall to form a sloping face – a feature also seen on the Garter and Salisbury Towers). This gave added strength to resist damage from missiles or mining tunnels and helped defenders fight back; missiles could be dropped from the walls to bounce off the batter

towards attackers. Above we see the narrow openings called arrow slits designed to give protection to archers while allowing them a reasonable view of attackers. The low wall around the castle mound, which further up the hill was removed and replaced by seats, can still be seen here.

On the far left is **No. 19 Thames St** (Prezzo) from the early/mid 1700s with segmental (curved top) windows typical of this earlier Georgian period. There is also a string course (raised decorative strip) between the first and second floors, a cornice (decorative moulding along the top) and a brick parapet (possibly a later addition) which hides attic dormer windows (not visible here). E V Tull ran a restaurant and confectioners (with Royal Warrants) here for many years.

Nos. 20 and 21 form a pair, also early 1700s (Georgian) with later alterations. Both show signs of structural distortion which adds charm. Each has a brick band between first and second floors, a cornice, a parapet and a mansard attic roof with a single dormer. On **No. 20** the roof is tiled and the windows are casements (opening on hinges) while **No. 21** has a slate roof and (vertically sliding) sash windows (*see View 8*). The wooden sash boxes (which hold the sash cords and window counterweights) are flush with the wall, an early design which was later banned to reduce fire risk. Regulations were introduced at first in London but later adopted more widely; from 1709 sash boxes had to be set back from the face and by 1774 hidden behind the brick work. **No. 22** is early 1800s (Regency) built from yellow (London stock) brick with recessed sash windows, a parapet and slate roof. **No. 23** is older, a timber framed building from the 1600s (Stuart) and altered in the early 1800s (Regency). The upper floors are jettied (overhanging the floor below).

47 Thames Street, River Street and Theatre Royal

From the base of the Curfew Tower we look towards the junction of Thames Street/River Street and beyond to Windsor Theatre.

On the far left **Nos. 24 and 25 Thames St**. (Zizzi) from the late 1700s (Georgian) was originally one house of 3 bays with the centre section projecting slightly. There is a brick parapet and tiled roof. The shop fronts are modern. No. 26, a grocers, and No. 27 the Red Lion public house on the corner were demolished in the 1920s and not replaced.

Next we come to **River Street** which leads from here to the Thames at a point where there was an ancient ferry crossing to Eton. The street has had several former names, originally New Street and then several confusingly similar names (probably alternative spellings) including Bier Lane and possibly Beer or Bear Lane. It changed to River Street in 1883.

Continuing across we come to **No. 28** (Thai Square) known as Keayne House and dated 1903 (Edwardian) with timber cladding in Jacobethan style – copying early 1600s features found on Elizabethan/Jacobean(James I) buildings. It has twin gables and jettied (overhanging) upper storeys with the original marble-faced butcher's shop front on the ground floor. It is now a restaurant. A plaque on the River Street side explains that a former house on this site was the birthplace in 1595 of Robert Keayne, who in 1638 went on to found the Ancient and Honourable Artillery Company of Massachusetts (USA). **No. 29** (Thai Square) was formerly the Adam and Eve public house, popular with patrons and performers at the nearby theatre and, like No. 28 next door, dates from about 1900 in Jacobethan style. The rear part is much older and a public house with the same name was here in the mid 1800s. **No. 30** (Bella Pasta) is part of the same building group, also early 1900s with twin gables topped by finials and mullioned windows on the first floor.

The **Theatre Royal** next door dates from 1910 (Edwardian) and though pleasant and inoffensive in style (with ashlar front, mullioned windows and decorated parapet) the facade seems to receive fairly dismissive comments on its architectural merit. Inside it is cosy and popular with theatregoers. The original theatre on this site was built in 1815 (Regency) and after ups and downs in its fortunes for nearly a century it suffered severe fire damage in 1908. The owner, Sir William Shipley, had sufficient funds to rebuild it. After a brief spell as a cinema in the 1930s it has continued as a theatre ever since.

The red brick building on the corner **No. 40** is from 1840 (early Victorian).

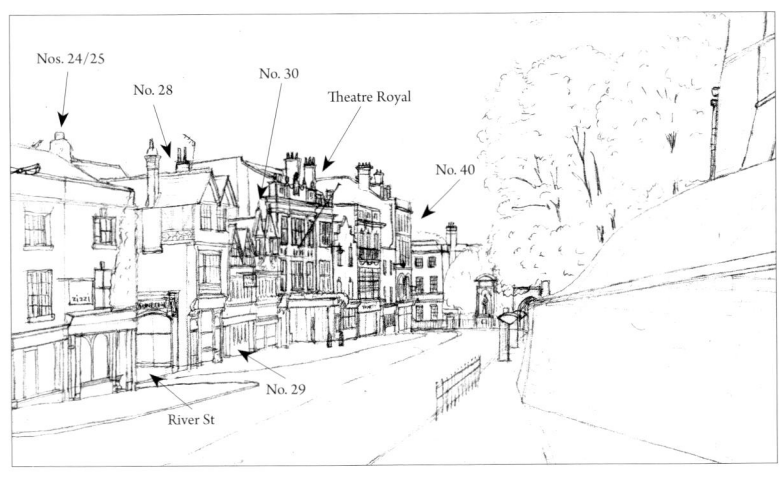

Nos. 24/25
No. 28
No. 30
Theatre Royal
No. 40
No. 29
River St

48 *Curfew Tower from River Street*

We look back towards Thames Street and the Curfew Tower from **River Street**, which has had many former names *(View 47)*. The Curfew Tower contains a belfry and bell chamber which extends into the roof. Since the bell chamber was built in 1479 (Edward IV – York) it has also housed a clock. The first two wore out but the third, with a mechanism to operate the chimes, is still in use, built (obviously very well) by John Davis, son of a Royal blacksmith, in 1689 (William III – Stuart). It plays the hymn tune *St David's* every three hours starting at 12 o'clock. When the tower was given its new roof in 1863 the clock was reinstalled but given a new face, the old one apparently hard to read. The bells, eight in number, can also be rung by hand in more complex patterns (changes), usually on special occasions. The small dormer-like gables allow the sound of the bells to radiate

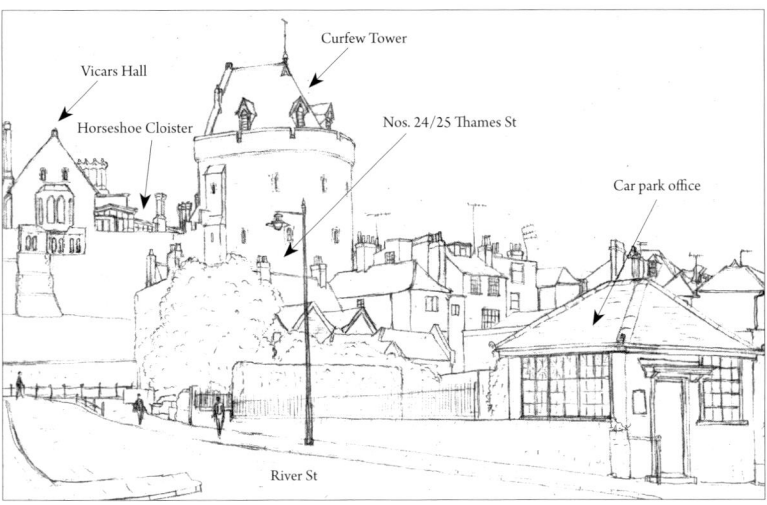

out from the tower. A larger gable on the other side of the roof houses the clock face *(View 43)*.

On the far left of the picture is the gable of the **Vicars Hall** built about 1415 (Henry V – Lancaster) as a Common Hall for the Priest Vicars of the College of St George who sang for the Chapel services. The projecting oriel window in Bath stone is a restoration by Anthony Salvin in 1864 (Victorian). To its right is the **Horseshoe Cloister**, built 1478/81 (Edward IV – York) and restored in 1871 by Sir George Gilbert Scott. The Cloister was built soon after work started on the new St George's Chapel to provide accommodation for the Priest Vicars. These singing men were transferred here from their accommodation on the other side of the lower ward which in 1557 under Mary I (Tudor) was to be occupied by the Poor (Military) Knights of the Order of the Garter *(View 31)*.

The side and rear of **Nos. 24/25 Thames Street** (Zizzi) are seen on the corner, partly obscured by a tree. To their left once stood No. 26 and No. 27 (Red Lion public house), demolished in 1926 as part of a slum clearance scheme. All the buildings lining this side of River Street along with smaller side streets were demolished, the street widened and **Windsor's first car park** was created in 1928. This survives (unsurprisingly), the former entrance/exit (now the exit) being just to the right of the picture. The building in the foreground (also 1928) served as a car park office. There is a larger two storey public toilet block in similar style further along the street which at one time also included a public bath house.

One of Windsor's many breweries (Jennings) was once located on the spot from which this view is seen. It is now (another) car park but when warehouse buildings were cleared from the site in 1987 an archaeological excavation (of Jennings Yard) revealed many historical artefacts.

49 *Thames Street, Castle Walls and the Hundred Steps*

From the corner of **River Street**/**Thames Street** the walls lining **the north side of the Lower Ward** are seen high above the street. This stretch is part of the stone wall created by Henry II (Plantagenet) in 1171/4 to replace the original wooden walls a century after the castle was founded by William I. The windows were added later, some during the restorations of the 1800s (Victorian). Behind the wall can be seen a Tudor half-timber/brick building with clusters of tall brick chimneys (these buildings, from various dates, are associated with the College of St George founded at the same time as the Order of the Garter by Edward III in 1348).

Like the upper parts of Thames Street, the side of the street beneath the castle would have been lined with buildings until the 1850s when they were cleared away (under the Town Improvement Act 1848). At the far end of the castle slope and just visible behind the trees, a sloping grey wall marks the position of a steep flight of steps called the **Hundred Steps** (though there are 134). These steps, probably originating in the 1300s, lead from the Canon's Cloister (part of the College of St George) in the Lower Ward down to the corner of Thames Street and were once a short cut from the castle to this part of the town. Following the clearance of the houses, the **Hundred Steps Lodge** was built by Anthony Salvin about 1860 (Victorian) *(View 51)* and the steps re-faced in stone. They are quite visible from the road but no longer in use.

No. 28 Thames Street (Keayne House) built in 1903 shows more detail of the Jacobethan half-timber effect described in *View 48*.

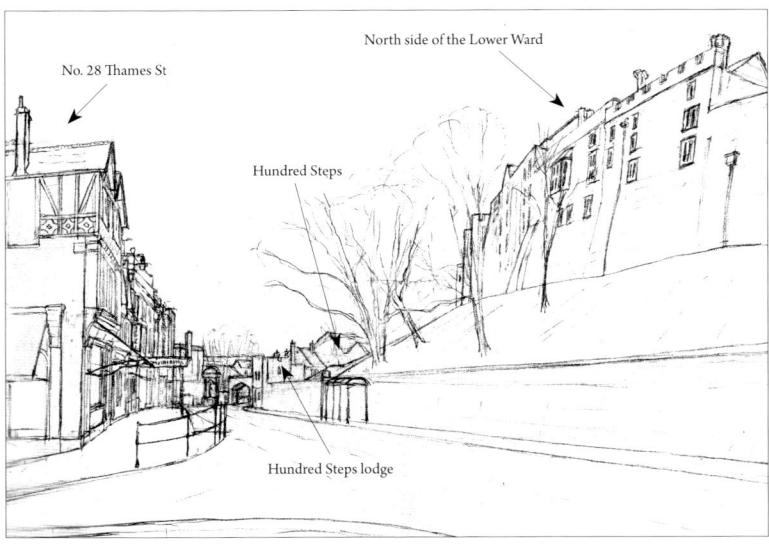

No. 28 Thames St

North side of the Lower Ward

Hundred Steps

Hundred Steps lodge

50 *Curfew Tower and Thames Street from Theatre Royal*

Looking back from the Theatre Royal we can appreciate the true height and impressive bulk of the Curfew Tower. Beyond, in the curve of Thames Street are visible a few buildings not covered in previous views.

Nos. 13/14 Thames Street (MacDonald's) is of similar date to **Nos. 15/17 The King and Castle** public house, originally built as a shop in 1917 by Boots the Chemist in Georgian revival style. To one side is **Boots Passage** (above which is a bust of Edward VII) named after Sir Jesse Boot who gave it as a right of way for public use. It leads down steps to an area called The Goswells (formerly the site of slum housing) purchased by

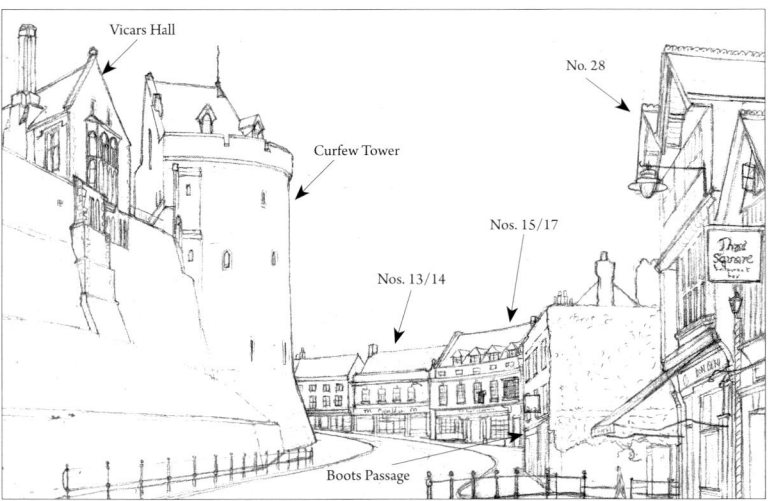

public subscription in 1910, and now in the care of the National Trust, to ensure that no building development would spoil views of the castle. In 2012 a garden and fountain were built here to commemorate the Diamond Jubilee of HM Queen Elizabeth II.

Some aspects of the **Curfew Tower** (roof, bells and battered base) are described in *Views 43, 46 & 48*. In the **basement** is a chalk-built room with vaulted ceiling from which leads a circle of deep alcoves. It may occasionally have served as a prison. Above is the **main floor**, with a door opening on to a mural (wall) chamber. From a trap door in this chamber leads a passage down to a secret route out of the castle called a sally port, created when this section of the castle was built in 1227/30. The tunnel carries on down chalk steps and into the old castle ditch but is now blocked off at the far end. **The upper floor** is filled with the huge belfry as previously described. Along with the other towers along the West End Wall it was refaced by Anthony Salvin in 1862/3 (Victorian) using Heath stone. The mechanical saws used to cut up the blocks created a neat but slightly stark appearance when compared to the original hand cut blocks still visible along the curtain walls. Heath stone is the name given to blocks of siliceous sandstone (containing silica), also called Sarsen stones, left on the land surface when glaciers melted after the last ice age. Similar stone was used for monuments such as Stonehenge in Wiltshire. It has the ability not only to self-clean but to reflect the mood of the day, shining bright in summer sunlight, gold in the evening sun and glowering grey on a dull winter's day.

The **Vicars Hall**, part of the College of St George within the castle walls and described in *View 48*, is seen on the far left.

On the right is **No. 28 Thames Street** (Keayne House) described in *View 47*.

51 *Old Bank House, Thames Street and Hundred Steps Lodge*

Old Bank House (formerly Bank House) stands near the point where Thames Street turns away from the castle and leads towards the river. It was built in 1758 (Georgian) for Henry Isherwood who owned a brewery close by in Datchet Lane (now Datchet Road). It served as both a brewery office and house for the owner. This elegant yellow brick building has many typical Georgian features including the centre section with (triangular) pediment, a cornice with brick modillions (small closely spaced brackets) and a doorway topped by a pediment and flanked by Doric columns. To its

left is an addition from the 1800s to provide a grand doorway to a side passage for the brewery. The brewery and house were sold to the Ramsbottom family about 1780 and John Ramsbottom, brewer and banker, established the Windsor Bank here, hence its name Bank House. In 1837 house and brewery passed to Neville Reid & Co. (also brewers and bankers), then to Noakes & Co and finally to brewers Courage & Co. The brewery closed in 1930 at the time of this final takeover though Courage still retained offices (and perhaps storage facilities) here until 1962. Part of the site was used to build the King George V Memorial in 1936/7 (*for information see View 52*). Old Bank House is now occupied by St George's School whose main building is nearby (*Views 55 & 56*).

To the right of Bank House is a **Statue of Prince Christian Victor** (grandson of Queen Victoria) who was born at Windsor Castle and killed in the Boer War (South Africa) in 1900. The bronze statue (1903) by Welsh sculptor Sir William Goscombe John was erected in his honour by friends, the surrounding niche and pedestal designed by A Y Nutt, architect and artist (Surveyor to the Dean and Canons of St George's).

Next is the **Hundred Steps Lodge** built by Anthony Salvin in 1860/62 as an entrance to the Hundred Steps which lead up to the Canons Cloister in the Lower Ward of the castle. The steps, which he rebuilt at the same time, are a steep and potentially treacherous short cut down to this part of the town. They are still quite visible but no longer used (*see also View 49*).

Above are the walls of the **North face of the Lower Ward** and buildings associated with the religious College of St George, founded in 1348 by Edward III (Plantagenet) at the same time as the Order of the Garter.

On the right the three storey building **No. 42 Thames Street** dates from 1830/40 (Regency) with a modern shop front. It is stuccoed (rendered) and has architraves (surrounds) around the windows, the centre one on the first floor flanked by pilasters (flat pillars). **Nos. 43/44** is a two storey, tiled roof building from the 1600s (Stuart) with a brick ground floor (and later alterations). The interior has mediaeval elements.

52 Bel & The Dragon and Datchet Road

The three gabled building on the corner of Thames Street and Datchet Road, now called **Bel & The Dragon** restaurant and tea room, was formerly the William IV public house. Its name prior to 1830, when William IV came to the throne, is not recorded. It was certainly William IV in 1837 (Regency/Victorian) and by 1910 the South Western Hotel (the latter name derived from the London & South Western Railway who built the nearby railway station) though it is not clear when the name changed. It later reverted back to the William IV which it remained until more recently when the usage changed from hotel/public house to restaurant. The timber-framed building dates from at least the 1600s (Stuart) and possibly 1500s (Tudor) with the upper floors jettied (overhanging).

The windows and doors are from the 1700s (Georgian) with a mix of sash (sliding) and casement (hinged) windows. On the Datchet Road side the windows have drip-moulds above and the doors are canopied. It is said that there has been a tavern on this site since mediaeval times.

To the left **No. 61 Thames Street** is a house with a stuccoed (rendered) late 1700s (Georgian) frontage (but later altered behind) – three storeys with a frieze and cornice below a tiled attic roof with dormers (originally two now four). Other features include lead downpipes and a sill band below the first floor windows.

Part of the building to the right of the restaurant **No. 5 Datchet Road** was occupied by Windsor's first telephone exchange in the early 1900s.

Windsor and Eton Riverside railway station is seen further down Datchet Road (*Views 53, 54 & 56*). Nearly opposite is the **Royal Oak** public house (*View 54*). Out of sight to the right of this view, on the opposite corner of Datchet Road/Thames Street, the **King George V memorial** designed by renowned British architect Sir Edwin Lutyens in Portland stone is from 1936 (unveiled 1937). It incorporates a central pedestal and fountains. When first built the site was quite open and light but is now rather gloomy, being overshadowed by large evergreen trees. It is on part of the site of the Windsor Brewery closed in 1930 (*View 51*).

No. 61 Thames St

Bel & The Dragon

No. 5 Datchet Rd

Royal Oak pub

Windsor & Eton Riverside station

53 *Windsor and Eton Riverside Railway Station*

Windsor was fortunate to acquire two grand railway stations, both termini, which also serve and include Eton in their titles. **Windsor & Eton Riverside station** seen here was completed in 1851 (Victorian) to replace a temporary structure erected in 1849 when the London and South Western Railway (LSWR) first arrived in Windsor. There had been great rivalry between the LSWR and the Great Western Railway (GWR) as to which would reach Windsor first and initially much opposition to both companies' plans from the Crown and Eton College. Attitudes to rail travel, significantly by Prince Albert and Queen Victoria, gradually changed and after much debate and various financial deals both arrived in 1849, with the GWR was just ahead. As well as a choice of regular services to London, it gave Windsor easy access to rail systems in two areas of Britain – the West Country and the South East – which, despite a thinning down of rail services nationally, it still enjoys today. *(See Views 40, 41 & 42 for information on the GWR Central Station).*

The LSWR, with their terminus at London Waterloo, approached Windsor via Staines and Datchet and needed to cross part of the Little Park, owned by the Crown, in order to build a station close to the town centre. The deal struck (requiring an Act of Parliament) allowed their line to enter Windsor close to the river along the edge of the Park. In return, the rail company funded new roads and bridges to carry traffic away from the castle. The new Datchet Road extended Windsor's Datchet Lane to Datchet across the new Victoria Bridge over the Thames (as well as an Albert Bridge between Datchet and Old Windsor) *(Map 11)*. This road cut through the Little Park (at this time renamed the Home Park) separating some of the land to the north near the river which the Crown, though still retaining ownership, designated as a recreation ground for the people of Windsor. The Home Park (Public) as it became known is still popular for sports and recreation to this day *(Views 58 and 59)*.

The station, designed by (Sir) William Tite, is in Neo-Tudor style (with features from buildings of the 1400/1500s) including buttresses and pointed Gothic arches with stone dressings. The red brick work includes dark blue/black bricks to create patterns (called diapering) The gabled **booking hall** is fronted by a giant bay window divided by mullions (vertical) and transoms (horizontal). Within, it contains an attractive wooden booking office – no longer in use because this part of the building is now a bar/restaurant. The **Royal Waiting Room** built for Queen Victoria is seen at the far end of the station. It is topped by a small lookout tower (with spirelet – small spire) used to warn of the Queen's approach from the castle to board the Royal Train.

Other interesting features on this side of the station are described in *View 56*.

Booking hall

Royal Waiting Room

54 *Windsor and Eton Riverside Station, Royal Oak and Castle from Farm Yard*

Windsor and Eton Riverside station is seen from the road called Farm Yard, between Thameside and Datchet Road. The roadway off to the left once led to the Goods (Freight) yard and Engine Shed all of which closed in the 1960s and the land turned into a car park. Along this side of the station were ex goods/parcels office buildings demolished in the early 1990s and replaced by the modern building on the left. The larger arch (now glassed in) was another entrance to the station concourse. Originally there were three platforms but one disappeared with the new developments. Other features of the station are described in *Views 53 & 56*.

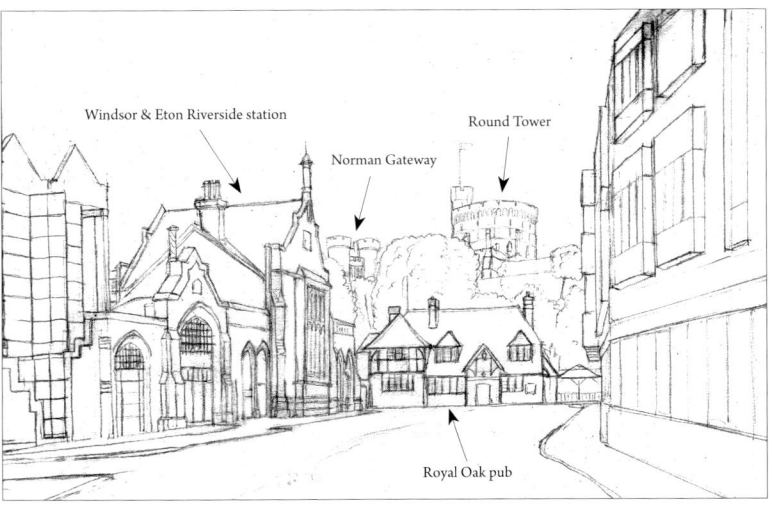

Windsor & Eton Riverside station

Norman Gateway

Round Tower

Royal Oak pub

Across the road is the **Royal Oak**. A public house of this name has been here for many years (at least the mid 1800s) but the present building dates from the 1930s in Mock Tudor/Tudorbethan style, typical of the period. It was at one time known as the Royal Oak Hotel, then Royal Oak and Railway Hotel but since 1935 just the Royal Oak (not hotel) so perhaps this indicates the building date. The Royal Oak as a pub name refers to the oak tree in which the future King Charles II hid when being pursued by Parliamentarian troops (Roundheads) after the Battle of Worcester in 1651, the final battle of the English Civil War. A few weeks later he escaped to France to live in exile. He returned in 1660 after the Interregnum period when the Commonwealth (the republic which replaced the Monarchy on the execution of Charles I in 1649) had gradually collapsed following Oliver Cromwell's death in 1658. Charles II was influenced by his life on the Continent (France, Netherlands) and some of the architectural styles he (and his architect Hugh May) saw would be reflected in subsequent changes at Windsor Castle.

The Windsor Brewery (*View 51*) which closed in 1930 was located behind the Royal Oak closer to the castle walls. Part of the brewery site to the right of the pub was later used for the George V memorial (*See View 52*). Beyond, we again see the castle's best known structure, the **Round Tower** described in *Views 5 & 31*.

To its left is a feature not yet described, the (inappropriately named) **Norman Gateway**. This is the main entrance to the Upper Ward from the Lower Ward and was built in 1360 (Edward III – Plantagenet). At about the same time a programme of rebuilding the Upper Ward was put in hand to create palatial accommodation. A large observation window was inserted in the left hand tower for Elizabeth I (Tudor) in 1583 at the end of the Long Gallery created for her between the Norman Gateway and the Henry VII tower (*View 59*). It was removed by Wyatville in 1830 (Regency) to restore some of the original design. The battlemented towers have between them a parapet with machicolations – open spaces between supporting brackets (corbels) through which objects or liquids could be dropped on to attackers.

55 *St George's School, Datchet Road and Winchester Tower from Riverside Station*

St George's School shares its origins with The College of St George and the Order of the Garter founded by Edward III (Plantagenet) in 1348. By 1352 the School comprised canons, vicars and six boy choristers who sang in St George's Chapel and was originally housed within the College of St George buildings inside the castle. Today the school is co-educational, teaching pupils from ages 4 to 13 with a choir-school still training young choristers. In 1893 (Victorian) the school moved down to the building seen here, known then as **Travers College**, founded by Samuel Travers who died in 1725

and in his will had set up a charitable institution for retired naval officers, run on similar lines to the Poor (Military) Knights of the Order of the Garter. They became known as Naval Knights. Due to legal problems the will was not validated until 1793 and the first appointments made in 1795. The college from 1803 (Georgian/Regency) is an elegant yellow (London stock) brick building with seven houses for the Knights and a mess house. A colonnade of (Greek inspired) Doric columns runs along the front and at each end is a projecting wing topped by a (triangular) pediment. In the centre is a bell tower with cupola (small dome) and weather vane. In 1892 the Institution was disbanded (for a variety of reasons including, over the years, misbehaviour and drunkenness by some of the Knights). A few were reluctant to leave and one was forcibly ejected in 1893.

The white painted buildings to the right of (and owned by) the school, **Nos. 7 and 8 Datchet Road**, are of similar age to the main building (early 1800s – Georgian/Regency). **No. 8** has a tiled mansard (attic) roof with dormers. Further down we see the **Royal Oak** public house (*View 54*).

Behind is the castle North wall with a number of unnamed projecting towers to the right but prominent is the **Winchester Tower** first built about 1170 by Henry II (Plantagenet) as an addition to the defences when the existing wooden structures were being replaced by stone. It was largely rebuilt in 1356/8 by William Wykeham, clerk of works to Edward III (see above). Wykeham oversaw the creation of palatial buildings in the Upper Ward from 1359 and built the bell tower for St George's Chapel – now the Mary Tudor Tower (*View 31*). He was later made Bishop of Winchester to whom the role of Prelate (of the Order of the Garter) was traditionally assigned. The Bishop lodged in the tower during the Garter gatherings, hence the name Winchester Tower. The tower was lived in by Sir Jeffry Wyatville during his remodelling of parts of the castle for George IV in the 1820/30s (Regency). Wyatville added a (projecting) oriel window and battlemented corner pieces but this tower still retains much of its appearance from the mid 1300s.

56 Datchet Road, St George's School and Riverside Station

We are in **Datchet Road** standing close to the Town Gate (*View 57*) which leads into the private part of the castle grounds, the Home Park (Private). The road was created in 1850/51 as a new route to Datchet (by continuing the existing Datchet Lane and building a new bridge over the Thames) as one condition of the deal struck when the London and South Western Railway brought its line into Windsor across Crown land. The old bridge over the Thames at Datchet was demolished at this time (*View 25*) (*Map 11*).

On the left is **St George's School**, the building originally created as Travers College (*View 55*).

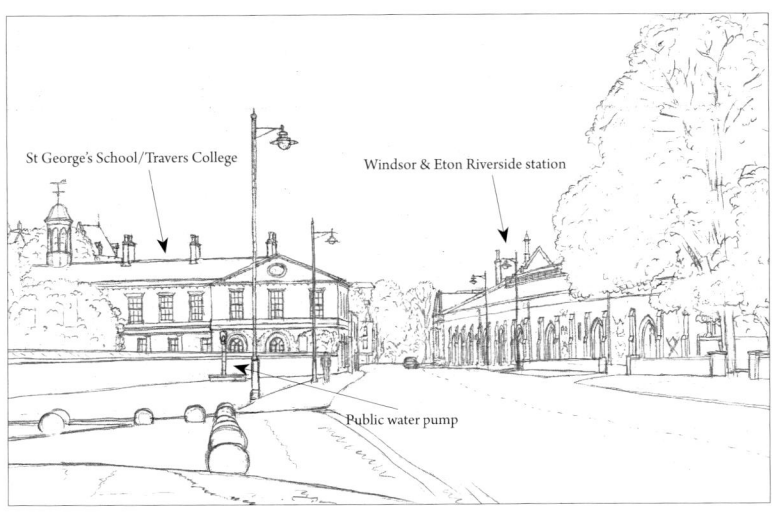

St George's School/Travers College

Windsor & Eton Riverside station

Public water pump

On the right is **Windsor and Eton Riverside** railway station (though the term 'train station' is now widely used). This was originally built by the London and South Western Railway – LSWR (*Views 53 & 54*). In 1923 the many independent railway companies of Britain were rationalised into four larger ones (known as The Grouping of the railways) and the LSWR joined the Southern Railway. The Central station (*Views 40, 41, 42*) joined the Great Western Railway – no name change because the largest and most important of the group gave its name to the new company. In 1948 after WWII (during which time the system was put under severe stress) the railways were reorganised again by being nationalised – taken under Government control to become British Railways. This process was reversed in 1993 when they were privatised. Currently the train service from the Riverside station is run by South West Trains while the track is nationally owned and maintained by Network Rail.

From this angle can be seen a number of unique features not before described. The row of tall blue doors was incorporated so that mounted soldiers of the Household Cavalry could pass through them and directly onto special trains, so speeding up the loading process. The brick work is decorated with diaper work, patterns created by dark blue/black bricks laid into the wall during construction, early examples of which can be seen at Eton College (founded in 1440 by Henry VI) and also in grand buildings of the Tudor period such as Hampton Court Palace. As well as Tudor-style diamond and chevron shapes there are initials; VR (Victoria Regina), PA (Prince Albert), SW (South Western), 1851 (the year the station was built) are seen in the picture but there are a few others including WT (William Tite – designer of the station) and WC (William Chaplin – Chairman of the LSWR).

Alongside the school wall on the left (in the picture just to the left of the tall lamp post) is the last **public water pump** built in Windsor in 1852 (Victorian) and sealed up in 1884 just before the Council acquired the local waterworks.

The Town Gate entrance is just out of sight to the left of the picture.

57 Town Gate

The building in the foreground is the lodge for the **Town Gate**, built in the mid-1800s (Victorian), which leads into the Home Park (Private). The history of the Home Park and its division into Home Park (Public) and Home Park (Private) is described in *View 58*. The gate is opposite the Royal Waiting room at the Riverside Station *(View 53)* and Queen Victoria would have exited the castle grounds here and travelled directly across to her train. The name Town Gate was originally given to a gate in Castle Street close to where the Advanced Gate is now located *(View 31)*.

The Home Park (Private) is now the venue for the Royal Windsor Horse Show (which had its origins in a Royal inspired wartime fund raising event staged in 1943 in the reign of King George VI, the present Queen's father) and which enjoys the full support and patronage of HM Queen Elizabeth II and the Royal family. As well as equestrian entertainment for all ages it includes international class show jumping and carriage riding. Prior to 2005 it was held in the Home Park (Public) but this area had always been susceptible to flooding and in wet years sometimes led to cancellation of events, or worse, the whole show. In 2005 it transferred to a purpose built all-weather area within the Home Park (Private). Since 2008 the Windsor Castle Royal Tattoo has provided military displays and music in the evenings following the daytime Horse Show events.

The Home Park (Public) is very popular for sporting purposes, recreation and dog walking. The Windsor Dog Show is still held here each year.

Above on the left is the **Round Tower** *(Views 5 & 31)*. The Royal Standard is flying, showing that HM Queen Elizabeth II is in residence at the castle. At other times the Union Flag (Jack) is flown. The Flag Officer is responsible for changing the flags when the Queen enters or leaves the castle. On special occasions, such as the Queen's birthday and on Garter Day, a much larger Royal Standard is flown.

Just to its left can be seen a tower of the **Norman Gateway** *(View 54)*. Between here and the large **Winchester Tower** on the right *(View 55)* is a small tower with two chimneys called the **Magazine Tower** (formerly Store Tower). It is mediaeval in origin but of uncertain date.

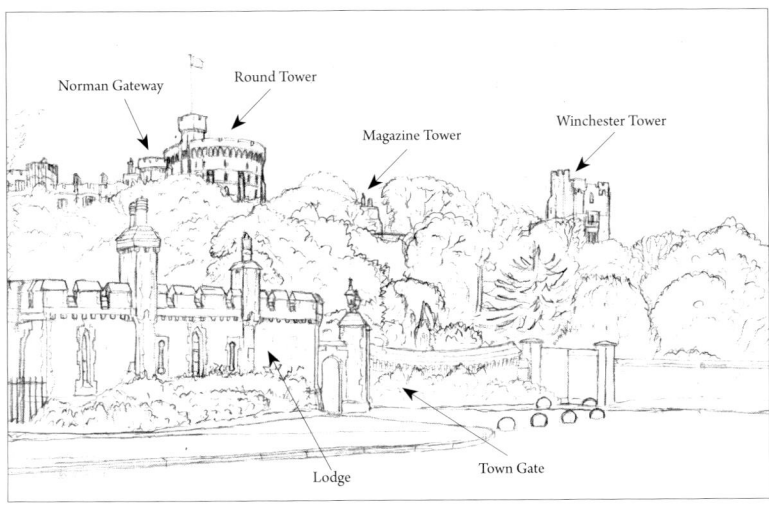

58 *Home Park and Castle in morning light*

This view is from the far side of the Home Park (Public), close to the railway line running into the Riverside Station. The full extent of the castle is well seen with the Upper Ward to the east (left), Lower Ward to the west (right) and between them the Middle Ward and Round Tower. On the right is the **Curfew Tower** roof. The other castle buildings are better seen and so are described in the similar but closer *View 59*. The **North Terrace**, a walkway in front of the northern buildings of the Upper Ward was first created as a wooden structure by Henry VIII (Tudor) in 1553/4 then rebuilt in stone by his daughter Elizabeth I in 1572. It was widened and extended for Charles II in 1674/80 and battlements added for George IV in the 1820/30s by Wyatville.

The Home Park (Public) was created about 1851 (Victorian) when the new

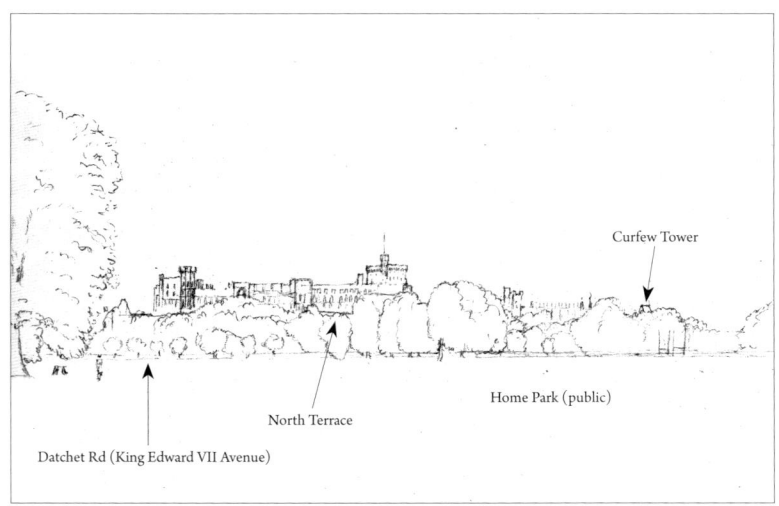

Datchet Road was built, largely funded by the London & South Western Railway on being allowed to bring its line into Windsor over Crown land *(View 53)*. Until this time the park area surrounding the castle was called the Little Park (to distinguish it from the much larger Great Park *(View 2)*. The new Datchet Road divided the Little Park into unequal parts which were renamed **Home Park (Private)**, the larger part around the castle, and **Home Park (Public)** the grassed area shown here. The public part is still owned by the Crown but designated as a recreation ground for the people of Windsor. The section of Datchet Road seen in the distance (where the dark green hedge runs across, beyond the dog walker) was later renamed King Edward VII Avenue (after the son and successor of Queen Victoria).

Going further back in history, until the late 1690s the old Datchet Lane in Windsor continued on across fields to the ferry crossing at Datchet. The Little Park (now Home Park) did not then include this land but in 1698 it was bought by William III, William of Orange (Stuart). He planned to build here a formal garden (to be called The Maastricht Garden after the 1673 Siege of Maastricht in the Franco-Dutch war). In preparation he built a brick wall around the edge of the now enlarged Little Park close to the river, leaving a new and more circuitous public roadway from Windsor to Datchet ferry between the wall and the river *(Map 11)*. He never started on the garden but from 1702 it was taken forward by his successor Queen Anne who created formal pathways, planted trees and built a lake (canal). She died before it was fully complete and her successor George I (who was not fond of Windsor) did not carry it further, after which it declined through lack of maintenance. Today, from ground level there is no trace of its former existence but in 1964 during a very dry summer an aerial photograph showed clearly where the garden, with its formal paths and lake, had been.

59 Home Park and Castle north front with cricket match

The north aspect of the castle is seen from west to east with structures from the foundation of the castle in 1070 to work from the 1800s. For the first time (in this book) are descriptions of buildings from the northern face of the Upper Ward with its Royal apartments which have seen many changes over the centuries as the castle evolved from fortress to palace. Some new works added to or altered the existing buildings; others obliterated what had gone before.

On the right is **St George's Chapel** begun in 1475 (Edward IV – York) to replace an earlier one already in use by the College of St George and the Order of the Garter

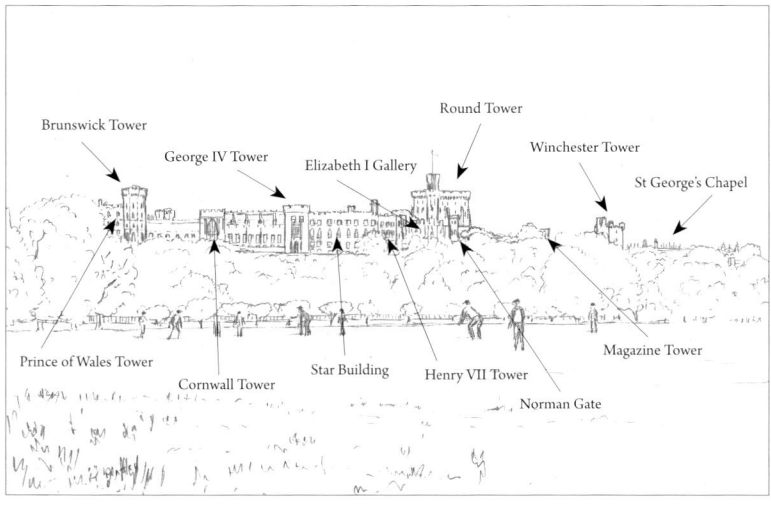

(both founded by Edward III in 1348). Completed in 1528 (Henry VIII –Tudor) it is one of the finest examples of English (Gothic) Perpendicular architecture. Next are the **Winchester Tower** (*View 55*) and **Magazine Tower** (*View 57*). On the **Castle Mound** from 1070 (William I) is the iconic outline of the **Round Tower** raised in height by Sir Jeffry Wyatville in 1828/32 (Regency) to dominate the skyline (*View 31*). From this vantage point the **Norman Gate** (*View 54*) and **Queen Elizabeth's Gallery** are seen in front of the Round Tower. This picture gallery was created for Elizabeth I (Tudor) in 1583/5 and a large observation window added to the Norman Gate. To its left the **Henry VII Tower** was added by that Monarch in 1499/50 (Tudor) as an extension of the Royal Lodgings.

The Star Building, 10 bays (windows) wide was a rebuild of existing apartments by Hugh May, architect to Charles II, in 1674/80 (Stuart) and so named for the giant Garter Star (an emblem of the Order of the Garter) decorating the centre of the wall. Later it was modified, first around 1800 for George III by James Wyatt (uncle of Wyatville) who changed windows from round to pointed Gothic arches. In the 1820s (Regency) Wyatville finished off the window replacement and created from part of it, on the east (left) side, the new **George IV Tower** forming an entrance into the new State Entrance Hall. This tower, with an oriel (projecting) window above, is now the public entrance to the State Apartments. From here on the buildings were either built or refaced by Wyatville – a seven bay mediaeval section (refaced 1830s), then the **Cornwall Tower** (created 1820/30s), **China Corridor, Brunswick Tower** (created 1820s). On the north east corner the **Prince of Wales Tower** was originally built by Henry II (Plantagenet) about 1170, but rebuilt by Anthony Salvin in 1853 (Victorian) after a fire. In 1992 a serious fire again broke out in this corner of the castle during renovation work causing damage to the Cornwall, Brunswick and Prince of Wales towers and many State apartments. The external faces were restored to their former appearance but within the castle were important changes such as a new ceiling for St George's Hall which had been largely destroyed.

60 Lower Thames Street and Sir Christopher Wren Hotel

Standing close to Windsor Bridge we look back along the lower part of Thames Street with **Old Bank House, Hundred Steps Lodge** and the castle walls *(View 51)* in the distance. Since the closure of Windsor Bridge *(Views 61 & 62)* to motorised traffic Lower Thames Street has been semi-pedestrianised, though vehicles are allowed for access.

On the far left **No. 57** is late 1700s (Georgian) and next door **No. 58** is mid-1700s, altered 1830/40 (Regency), both with modernised shop fronts. Beyond is the projecting window of **Gainsborough House** (1985) with neo-Tudor features. From 1928 to 1983 there was a cinema here, the last of many in the town, which had

been sympathetically designed to blend in with the Georgian buildings on either side.

The **Sir Christopher Wren Hotel** (with the white porch) is on the right. Sir Christopher Wren, designer of St Paul's Cathedral in London, had connections with Windsor in that his father was Dean and the young Christopher may have spent time here. Sir Christopher's son, also Christopher, was later a Member of Parliament for Windsor *(View 15)*. It has been claimed that this building was designed and lived in by Sir Christopher in the late 1600s but current opinion favours the mid-1700s (Georgian) as a more likely building date; Wren died in 1723. It was probably built for a brewer/distiller named Robert Moore. The **main building** is seven bays (windows) wide, the centre projecting section topped by a (triangular) pediment with modillions (brackets). There is a prominent (Roman inspired) Doric porch with plain columns and triglyph (three groove) patterns around the frieze. The **building to its left**, once a separate house, is now a wing of the hotel. It is from late 1700s with a slate mansard attic roof (and dormers) and on the right side a loggia (covered passage) leading to an alternative access door. The street door, flanked by pilasters (flat pillars), has a fanlight above. **The painted brick building on the far right** (also a wing of the hotel) is from the early 1800s (Regency).

Nos. 50/51 Thames Street, the yellow (London stock) brick building from 1830/40 (Regency) was originally one house later converted into two dwellings, both with shop fronts. Beyond, the yellow painted building **No. 49 Thames Street** (now Olivia Café at the front and Wrens Club – part of the hotel – to the rear) was until the 1990s a public house called **The Swan** (Inn). This former coaching inn (not all of which survives) dates from at least the 1500s (Tudor) but was re-fronted in the early 1800s (Regency). The side passage (through which coaches would have passed) still reveals some of the original timber frame and brick infilling (nogging). In 1803 (Georgian/Regency) it was the meeting place of an exclusive dining club, the Windsor Monthly Club, and seems to have been popular with the better off drinkers and diners of Windsor.

61 *Windsor Bridge from the River Thames*

We are standing on the riverside walkway by the Thames looking towards **Windsor Bridge** with Eton on the far side. The building on the far right is part of the Sir Christopher Wren Hotel *(View 60)* next to which the steps lead down from Thames Street to the riverside promenade.

There was a bridge here across the River Thames by at least the 1200s and probably earlier (1172 is sometimes quoted), not long after the town of New Windsor was established around the castle in the early 1100s. The wooden structure was replaced many times over the centuries with tolls charged to assist with its upkeep *(View 25)*. By the early 1800s a decision was made to replace the existing wooden bridge with something more substantial using modern technology.

Eton

In 1822 (Regency) Charles Hollis, who had recently designed the new Parish Church using cast-iron supports for the roof *(View 14)*, was asked by Windsor Corporation to draw up plans for the new bridge. Thomas Telford, an experienced engineer and bridge designer, was consulted by Hollis but probably only advised on the foundations rather than the bridge itself. The structure is supported on granite pillars set deep into the river bed between which are three arches each formed from seven cast-iron sections across the width of the bridge. It bears the Windsor Coat of Arms at each end. Opened in 1824 at a cost of £15,000, the bridge continued to provide the main route north from Windsor through Eton High Street to the Bath Road at Slough. To assist with the building costs Windsor Corporation was authorised by Parliament to collect tolls for a period of 21 years. Tolls were still being charged into the 1890s despite many unsuccessful attempts from the 1860s onwards to get them withdrawn. In 1896 Joseph Taylor, an Eton resident, paid his toll charge and then issued a writ to recover the money. After a long legal battle the House of Lords declared that the collecting of tolls on this bridge was now unlawful and in December 1898 they were withdrawn. A plaque on the bridge commemorates Joseph Taylor's action.

In the 1900s with increasing traffic volumes and vehicle weights the bridge was subjected to stresses for which it had not been designed and by 1970, when cracks were found in the cast iron supports, it was closed to motorised traffic. Fortunately a new Thames crossing, the Elizabeth Bridge, had been opened in 1966 on the edge of the town as part of a new Windsor Relief Road (a bypass route to Slough and the fledgling M4 motorway) so reducing the inconvenience that might otherwise have been caused. Though the vehicular route between Windsor and Eton is now more circuitous the bridge still provides a direct link for pedestrians and cyclists.

62 *Windsor Bridge from Eton*

This view from the side of **Windsor Bridge** looks back across the Thames from Eton to Windsor. The lamp in the foreground is a relatively modern replacement for a previous design. The cast-iron bridge with granite support pillars, now pedestrianised, is described in *View 61*.

The river is now used mainly for pleasure rather than commerce. Boats pass through Windsor frequently during the summer months and there are also many small craft for hire locally, but at one time the riverside near the bridge was lined with wharves and warehouses some serving the town's breweries. After many changes of ownership and takeovers, the Windsor Brewery located in Datchet Road run by Noakes & Co.

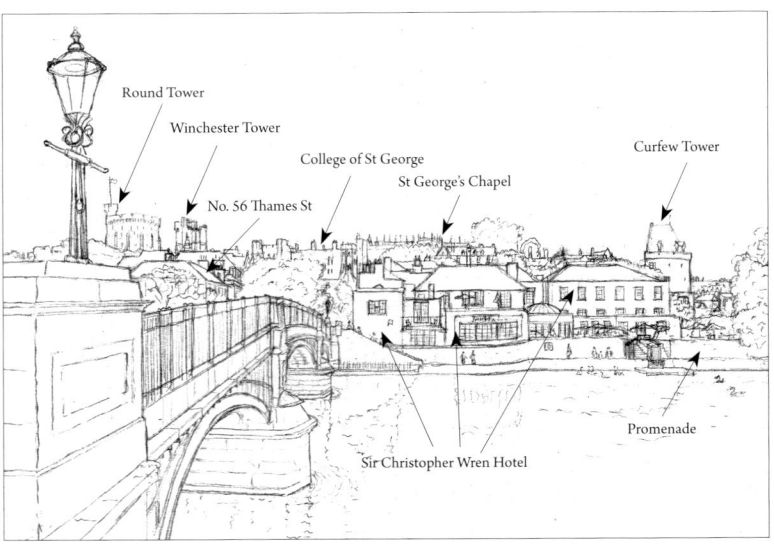

was bought out by Courage & Co in 1930 and immediately closed down *(View 51)*. Windsor's last brewery, Burge and Co. in Victoria Street, closed a year later in 1931 so ending a tradition which had been one of its most important industries. However, since 2010 the new Windsor & Eton Brewery which opened a short way out of the town centre has met with success supplying good real ales to many local establishments.

The present **promenade** was begun in the early1900s with the creation of Barry Avenue (after Sir Francis Tress Barry who made a fortune from a copper mine in Portugal and was Member of Parliament for Windsor in the 1890s) and was completed as far as the bridge by the 1930s.

Beyond the promenade are the buildings of **Sir Christopher Wren Hotel** *(View 60)* with those seen here (to the rear of the main building) having been altered during the 1900s. On the other side of the bridge (just behind the woman dressed in red) is **No. 56 Thames Street** (also part of the hotel) a building from about 1830 (Regency) and with a river frontage. It has French windows opening onto an 1850 (Victorian) veranda balcony.

On the skyline from left to right can be seen parts of the castle – the **Round Tower** *(View 31)*, **Winchester Tower** *(View 55)* **walls of the College of St George on the north front** *(View 51)* **St George's Chapel** *(View 59)* and far right the **Curfew Tower** *(Views 43, 48 & 50)*.

63 *Windsor from The Rafts, Eton*

This view looks across to Windsor from The Rafts boathouses located on The Brocas, a meadow on the Eton side of the river owned by Eton College but freely accessible for public recreation. In the foreground on the left are The Rafts, a name given to the boathouses dating from 1899 (Victorian/Edwardian) which until 2006 were used by Eton College as the base for its pupils rowing on the river. In 2006 the Eton Rowing Lake opened, close to the river about 3 miles (5 km) upstream near the village of Dorney. This world class facility is used by pupils but is also made available for national and international rowing events. It was the rowing venue for the 2012 Olympic and Paralympic Games. In 2013 the majority of The Rafts buildings were demolished to be replaced by housing.

The view of Windsor shows many of the structures on the northern side of the castle and the town. Taking the castle first, on the far left is the **Brunswick Tower** on the corner of the Upper Ward (*View 59*), a turret on the **Star Building** (*View 59*), the **Norman Gateway** (*Views 54 & 57*), the **Magazine Tower** (*View 57*) the **Round Tower** (*Views 31, 54 & 57*), and in front the **Winchester Tower** (*Views 55 & 57*), **north face of the Lower Ward with buildings of the College of St George** (*View 49 & 51*), **St George's Chapel** (*View 59*), **Vicars Hall** and **Horseshoe Cloister** (*Views 48 & 50*) and the **Curfew Tower** (*Views 43, 48 & 50*). The true size and splendour of St George's Chapel in relation to the castle in which it stands can be appreciated from this vantage point.

In front, some of the buildings of the town can be seen. On the left buildings of the **St Christopher Wren Hotel** and **Gainsborough House** in Thames St (*View 60*), the back of the **Theatre Royal** (*View 47*) and **Brown's Restaurant** on the corner of River Street and Barry Avenue which dates from about 1906/7 (formerly the Thames Hotel, then The Old Trout pub/music venue then the Fort & Ferkin pub).

On the river a French Brothers boat is moored to take on passengers for a trip up river, the regular shorter trips being to Boveney Lock and back.

The trees on the right of the picture are on a small island called Firework Ait.

The birds in the foreground are Mute Swans (*Cygnus olor*), Canada Geese (*Branta canadensis* and Mallard Ducks (*Anas platyrhynchos*).

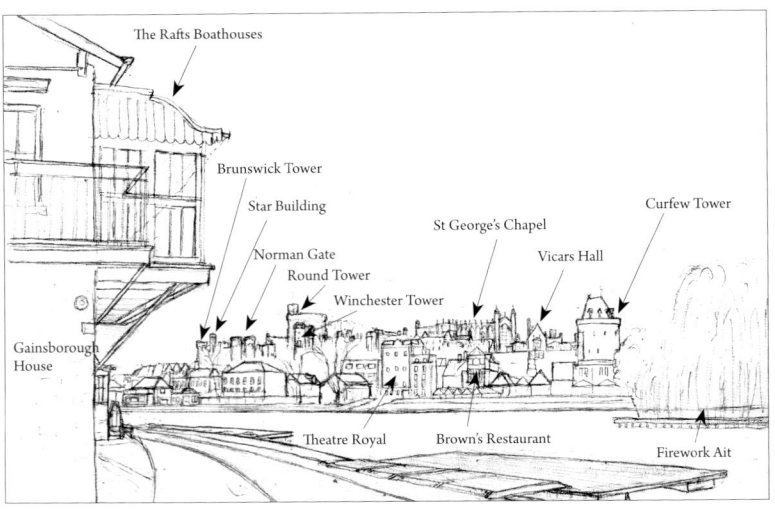

64 *Windsor Castle and the River Thames from the Island*

Windsor Castle forms a splendid backdrop to this view seen from an island in the Thames, on which stands one of the abutments of the rail bridge built by the Great Western Railway (GWR), and designed by I K Brunel to carry their branch line from Slough to Windsor. The line is now single track but the original Victorian bridge, not pictured in this book, survives. *(See Views 43, 44, 45 for GWR information)*

On the left shore is **The Brocas**, an ancient meadow owned by Eton College but open for public recreation. In the summer months private boats are often moored along this stretch, as well as on the Windsor side. On the right is the **promenade next to Barry Avenue** *(View 62)* from which small craft can be hired and trips taken on larger pleasure boats operated by French Brothers and (just beyond Windsor bridge) Salter's Steamers *(View 6)*.

In the foreground is a group of Mute Swans *(Cygnus olor)* which, together with many species of duck, Canada Geese *(Branta canadensis)* and other water birds, are found in large numbers along this stretch of the Thames. The fact that they are often fed by visitors provides an incentive to stay in the area. Swan Lifeline is a charity based on the Eton side of the river which cares for sick or injured swans.

All swans living on a 70 mile (113 km) stretch of the Thames, including Windsor, are the property of one of three owners – either the Sovereign or one of two designated Worshipful Companies, the Dyers and the Vintners (the latter two being ancient livery companies who, in mediaeval times, were granted rights to own some of the swans). The ownership of swans originated in Norman times when some were used as high class banquet food for the Royal table. An ancient ceremony called Swan Upping is still carried out each year to keep a check on the numbers and health of the population. Each July the Queen's Swan Marker oversees the five day trip from Sunbury (in the old county of Middlesex) to Abingdon (Oxfordshire) accompanied by 19 Swan Uppers in three teams. All wear special ceremonial uniforms. The swans are checked and weighed and some cygnets (young swans) have a marker ring placed on one of their legs. Traditionally the Sovereign's swans are unmarked while those of the two companies are distinctively ringed. Cygnets follow the ownership previously allotted to their parents; cygnets from Vintners' swans are themselves given Vintners' rings during the ceremony, the Monarch's remain unmarked and so on.

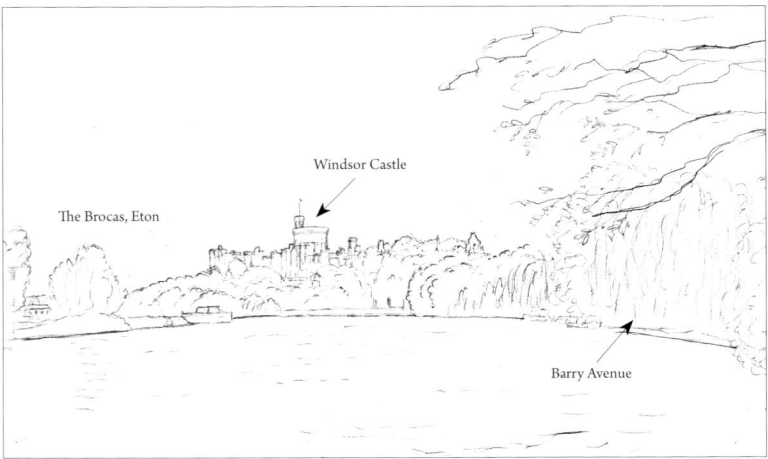

The Brocas, Eton

Windsor Castle

Barry Avenue

References

Books, Guides & Maps

Marshall's Guide to Windsor

Kelly's Guide to Windsor (various dates)

Windlesora *Windsor Local History Group* (various dates)

Windsor in Victorian Times *Angus MacNaghton* 1975

Windsor and Eton in Georgian Times
Angus MacNaghton 1976

The Book of Windsor *Raymond South* 1977

The Story of Windsor *Maurice Bond* 1984

The Guards *Pitkin Guide* 1990

Around Windsor in Old Photographs *Beryl Hedges* 1992

Old Ordnance Survey Maps – Windsor 1897, Windsor Castle
& Datchet 1897 *Alan Godfrey Maps* 1994

The Buildings of Windsor *Richard K Morriss* 1994

Windsor Castle *Olwen Hedley* 1994

Views of Windsor *Jane Roberts* 1995

A Millennium in the Royal Borough
Luke Over and Chris Tyrrell 1999

Windsor Castle – The Official Illustrated History
John Martin Robinson 2001

Windsor – A Thousand Years *Windsor Local History
Publications Group* 2001

Windsor – Centuries of Change *Sheila Rooney* 2002

Britain's Historic Railway Stations *Gordon Biddle* 2003

Georgian London *John Summerson* 2003

Streets of Windsor & Eton *edited by Bridgette Mitchell*
(Windsor Local History Publications Group) 2003

The Great Park and Windsor Forest *Clifford Smith* 2004

Britain in Old Photographs – Around Windsor & Eton
Michael Stiles 2004

Georgian and Regency Houses Explained *Trevor Yorke* 2007

Windsor – Fun, Facts, History and Legend
Caroline Wagstaff 2009

Vanished Windsor *compiled by Elias Kupfermann*
(Windsor Local History Group) 2010

Windsor Great Park – A Visitor's Guide *Andrew Fielder* 2010

The Buildings of England – Berkshire *Geoffrey Tyack, Simon Bradley*
and Nikolaus Pevsner 2010

Windsor Guildhall History and Tour *Pamela Marson and*
Bridgette Mitchell 2011

Windsor Eton and the Neighbourhood – A Visitor's Guide
Andrew Fielder 2011

Old Ordnance Survey Maps – Windsor (North) 1868,
Windsor (South) 1868 *Alan Godfrey Maps* 2011

The Royal Line of Succession *Hugo Vickers* 2012

Windsor Through Time *The Friends of Windsor & Royal
Borough Museum* 2013

Historical Map of Windsor About 1860 *researched and
compiled by David Lewis (Historic Towns Trust)* 2013

Internet

www.stgeorges-windsor.org

en-wikipedia.org

www.royal.gov.uk

www.royalcollection.org.uk

www.berkshirehistory.com

www.windsor.gov.uk

www.breweryhistory.co.uk

www.britishlistedbuildings.co.uk

www.english-heritage.org.uk

www.thamesweb.co.uk

www.british-history.ac.uk

www.quickiwiki.com

theroyalwindsorforum.yuku.com

itunes/apple/com/app *Capturing Windsor Castle – Watercolour paintings
by Paul and Thomas Sandby from the Royal Collection*

Acknowledgements

Thanks also to John Briscoe for information on the history of
Wistaria House, Kings Road and its architect Stephen Salter Junior.
Special thanks to Maggie Aldred (designer) without whose skill,
advice and patience this book would not have been possible.

British Library Cataloguing in Publication Data
A catalogue record of this book is available from the British Library
ISBN 978-0-9932468-0-7

Text, illustrations and maps: copyright © Jeff Sanderson 2015
Designed by Maggie Aldred
Published by Curfew Publishing
www.curfewpublishing.co.uk Contact: info@curfewpublishing.co.uk

Printed by Short Run Press